ACKNOWLEDGEMENTS

ACCA acknowledges the guidance and diligence provided by the diverse expertise embodied in the membership of the 2015 QI Specification Review Committee:

CONTRACTORS	Ellis Guiles (HT Lyons; Allentown, PA) Ted Konechne (Tempo Mechanical Services; Irving, TX) Rob Minnick (Minnicks; Laurel, MD) John Van Horne (Arundel Cooling and Heating; Linthicum, MD) Eric Woerner (Direct Energy US Home Services; Miamisburg, OH)
UTILITY	Scott Higa (Southern California Edison; Rosemead, CA) Marshall Hunt (Pacific Gas & Electric; Davis, CA) Bill Snyder (Duke Energy; St. Petersburg, FL)
OEMS	Jeff Cross (WaterFurnace International; Fort Wayne, IN) Gary Georgette (Carrier Corp.; Indianapolis, IN) Ray Granderson (Rheem Manufacturing; Fort Smith, AR) Hung Pham (Emerson Climate Technologies; Sidney, OH)
ASSOCIATIONS	Hugo Aguilar (IAPMO; Ontario, CA) Luis Escobar (ACCA; Arlington, VA) Eli Howard (SMACNA; Chantilly, VA) John Jones (BPI; Malta, NY) Lauren Liecau (CEE; Boston, MA) Warren Lupson (AHRI; Arlington, VA) Shawn Martin (ICC; Pittsburgh, PA)
GOV.	Dean Gamble (U.S. EPA ENERGY STAR; Washington, DC) Brent Ursenbach (Salt Lake County; Salt Lake City, UT) Iain Walker (Lawrence Berkley National Laboratory; Berkley, CA) Martin Weiland (U.S. General Services Administration; Arlington, VA)
TRAIN.	Jack Rise (Jack Rise HVAC Technical Training; Tampa, FL) Dave Swett (Real World HVAC Inc; Shelby, NE)
ALLIED	Kristin Heinemeier (UC Davis Western Cooling Efficiency Center; Davis, CA) Mike Lubliner (WSU Energy Program; Olympia, WA) Lou Marrongelli (Conservation Service Group; Albany, NY) Bill Spohn (TruTech Tools; Akron, OH) Dennis Stroer (Calcs-Plus; North Venice, FL)

ACCA gratefully acknowledges the direction, guidance and encouragement provided by the diverse expertise embodied in the membership of the QI Specification Review Committee (2010) and QI Specification Development Committee (2007):

	2010 Review Committee	2007 Development Committee
CONTRACTORS	Richard Dean (Environmental System Associates) Ellis Guiles (TAG Mechanical Systems) Stan Johnson (Stan's Heating and Air Conditioning) Skip Snyder (Snyder Company) Larry Taylor (Air Rite Air Conditioning) Eric Woerner (Airtron)	Robert Feathers (B. F. Mechanical) Gregory J. Goater (Isaac Heating & Air Conditioning) Joe Presley (Tri-City Mechanical) Larry D. Sambrook (Indoor Air Quality Network) Mitchell Slavensky (ACS Controls) Skip Snyder (Snyder Company)
UTILITY PROG. ADMINISTRATORS	Paul Kyllo (Southern California Edison) Buck Taylor (Roltay)	John Jones (NYSERDA) David P. Manoguerra (Pacific Gas & Electric) Christopher Neme (VEIC/NEEP) R. Anthony Pierce (Southern California Edison) Michael G. Stephens (TXU Electric Delivery) Buck Taylor (Massachusetts CoolSmart)
OEMs	Manny Cano (Lennox) Daniel L. Ellis (Climate Master) Gary E. Georgette (Carrier) Raymond Granderson (Rheem) Joe C. Leonard, Jr. (Allied Air Enterprises) Chris Mann (Water Furnace International) Hung M. Pham (Emerson) Bill Spohn, P.E. (TruTech Tools)	Gary E. Georgette (Carrier) Raymond Granderson (Rheem) Joe C. Leonard, Jr. (Allied Air Enterprises) James W. Muncie (American Standard) Hung M. Pham (Emerson)
ASSOCIATIONS & OTHERS	Chris Granda (Grasteu Associates) Glenn C. Hourahan, P.E. (ACCA) Ted Leopkey (EPA) Michael Lubliner (WSU – Energy Program) Warren Lupson (AHRI) Patrick L. Murphy (NATE) Harvey M. Sachs, Ph. D (ACEEE) Frank Stanonik (AHRI) John Taylor (CEE)	Glenn C. Hourahan, P.E. (ACCA) Patrick L. Murphy (NATE) William J. Parlapiano, III (BPI) Harvey M. Sachs, Ph. D. (ACEEE) Frank Stanonik (GAMA) John Taylor (CEE) Chandler von Schrader (EPA Energy Star)

ADDITIONAL ACKNOWLEDGEMENTS

This document has received helpful comments and input from numerous knowledgeable individuals from the 2007 development through the 2015 update. These included:

Jerry Adams (TXU Electric Delivery; Dallas, TX)

Mark M. Anderson (Cortez Heating & Air Conditioning, Inc; Bradenton, FL)

Ron Bladen (Fairfax County Code Specialist II; Fairfax, VA)

Linda Cavalluzzi (Long Island Power Authority; Long Island, NY)

George Chapman (Consortium for Energy Efficiency; Boston, MA)

Christine Colditz (Laco Mechanical Services; Elk Grove Village, IL)

Wes Davis (Air Conditioning Contractors of America; Arlington, VA)

David Dugger (Shoffner Mechanical & Industrial; Knoxville, TN)

Janis Erickson (Sacramento Municipal Utility District; Sacramento, CA)

Glenn Friedman, P.E. (Taylor Engineering; Alameda, CA)

James E. Gilroy (PacifiCorp; Portland, OR)

Ellis G. Guiles, Jr. P.E. (TAG Mechanical Systems, Inc.; Syracuse, NY)

Sally Hamlin (US EPA, Stratospheric Protection Division; Washington. DC)

Jeff Hammond (Enertech Manufacturing, LLC; Greenville IL)

Quinn Hart, P.E. (Head Quarters Air Force Civil Engineers; Tyndall AFB, FL)

Glenn Hourahan, P.E. (ACCA; Arlington, VA)

Larry Jeffus (Consultant to TXU Electric Delivery; Dallas TX)

Scott Jones (GeoSystems LLC (A subsidiary of Research Products Corp; Maple Grove, MN)

Lawrence Johnson (U.S. Air Force; Minot, ND)

Tom Kavounas (Albemarle Heating & Air; Charlottesville, VA)

Joseph Kounen (Building Performance Institute; Malta, NY)

Warren Lupson (Lupson & Associates; Silver Spring, MD)

Xiaobing Liu, Ph.D. (Oak Ridge National laboratory; Oak Ridge, TN)

Kevin B McCray (National Ground Water Association; Westerville, OH)

Michael McLaughlin (Southland Industries; Dulles, VA)

Lisa Meline, P.E. (Meline Engineering Corporation; Sacramento, CA)

Arthur T. Miller (Community College of Allegheny County; Pittsburgh, PA)

Wayne W. Mulholland (Tri County Mechanical; Azle, TX)

John Parker (retired: Alabama Power Company; Verbena, AL)

Donald Prather (Air Conditioning Contractors of America; Arlington, VA)

John Proctor (Proctor Engineering Group; San Rafael, CA)

Maggie Ramos (Long Island Power Authority, Long Island, NY)

Thomas A. Robertson (Baker Distributing Company; Jacksonville, FL)

Leslie Sandler (consultant; Fairfax Station, VA)

Dick Shaw (Air Conditioning Contractors of America; Arlington, VA)

Bruce Silverman (Airite Air Conditioning; Tampa, FL)

William W. Smith (Elite Software; College Station, TX)

David Swett (HVAC Training Center; Omaha, NE)

Neil Sybert (San Diego Gas & Electric; San Diego, CA)

Surumi J. Thorpe-Hudacsko (Silver Spring, MD)

Peter M. Van Lancker (Rheem Air Conditioning; Fort Smith, AR)

Martin J. Weiland, P.E. (Alexandria, VA)

Richard F. Welguisz (Trane; Tyler, TX)

Richard Wirtz (Heating, Airconditioning & Refrigeration Distributors International; Columbus, OH)

Tom Yacobellis (Ductbusters Incorporated; Dunedin, FL)

FOREWORD

[This Foreword is not part of the Standard. It is merely informative and does not contain requirements necessary for conformance to the Standard. It has not been processed according to the ANSI requirements for a standard and may contain material that has not been subject to public review or a consensus process. Unresolved objectors on informative material are not offered the right to appeal at ACCA or ANSI.]

Market Awareness
A significant market opportunity for improving the quality of HVAC equipment installations and service involves raising the awareness of consumers and building owners / operators about the benefits provided by professional contractors following industry-recognized quality installation practices (e.g., correct equipment selection, installation, and commissioning). Building owners / operators and residential consumers need to be informed of the links between comfort, humidity levels, utility bills, indoor air quality, and with a proper HVAC system design and installation. Once aware, consumers will better understand the value of a quality installation (QI) from their HVAC contractor. Consumers and building owners/operators who understand QI will also help position consumers and building owners / operators to consider the complete value-to-cost equation, not merely the "first price," when making HVAC equipment purchasing decisions. Customers who select contractors that promote QI and high performance HVAC equipment enjoy enhanced comfort, reduced energy usage, improved occupant productivity, and enhanced occupant safety.

Industry Need
There is a need to establish a performance bar to improve the core competencies of contractors to ensure that quality installations occur. This is beneficial not only as a process improvement for HVAC businesses, but, more importantly, for fulfilling the needs of building owners/operators in quality installations – comfortable, safe, energy-efficient indoor environments. This Standard provides a universally accepted definition for quality installation across a broad spectrum of the HVAC industry (e.g., manufacturers, distributors, contractors, user groups, customers, utilities, efficiency advocates, trade associations, professional societies, and governmental agencies).

Full observance of the quality installation elements may increase the initial "first cost" to the residential or commercial building owner/operator. However, the increased "value" – resulting from improved energy efficiency, better comfort, enhanced indoor air quality (IAQ), improved equipment reliability, longer equipment life, etc. – is expected to far exceed any added upfront price. Additionally, adherence to the elements in this specification provides intangible societal benefits in the form of reduced power grid energy demand that aids in reducing pollution and dependence on foreign oil.

Standard Intent
This Standard is written with the intent that various HVAC industry stakeholders may use the criteria in diverse manners for new construction as well as replacement applications. Examples include:
- Contractors – to demonstrate their commitment to quality HVAC installations in residential and commercial building applications;
- Equipment manufacturers – to highlight and encourage quality contractor practices, resulting in better equipment performance and durability;
- HVAC trainers – to assist in the ongoing development of appropriate course curricula and training programs;
- Utilities – to integrate the requirements into their incentive programs;
- Building owners/operators – to identify quality contractor practices and to ensure that quality installations are received;
- Certification bodies – to develop performance-based personnel certifications for individuals installing and maintaining HVAC equipment.

INTRODUCTION

[This Introduction is not part of the Standard. It is merely informative and does not contain requirements necessary for conformance to the Standard. It has not been processed according to the ANSI requirements for a standard and may contain material that has not been subject to public review or a consensus process. Unresolved objectors on informative material are not offered the right to appeal at ACCA or ANSI.]

In this Standard, the QI elements focus on the application and how well the system is selected and actually installed. QI is more than just using high-efficiency products and systems. The correct design, proper installation, and final testing have a large impact on occupant satisfaction and energy savings. [Quantification of energy penalties from not observing the QI elements are detailed in a research investigation completed September 2014 by the National Institute of Standards and Technology; available as a free download from www.acca.org/quality.]

For this Standard, core areas that characterize a quality installation include:

Design Aspects:
- Ventilation
- Building heat gain/loss load calculations
- Proper equipment capacity selection
- Geothermal heat pumps ground heat exchanger
- Matched systems

Equipment Installation Aspects:
- Airflow through indoor heat exchangers
- Water flow through heat exchangers
- Refrigerant charge
- Electrical requirements
- On-rate for fuel- fired equipment
- Combustion venting system
- System controls

Distribution Aspects:
- Duct leakage
- Airflow balance
- Hydronic balance

System Documentation and Owner Education Aspects:
- Proper system documentation to the owner
- Owner/operator education

The requirements of this Standard are applicable to all equipment included in the Scope Sections §2.1 (Equipment Types) and §2.2 (Equipment Systems/Components). The requirements are equally applicable to minimum- through high-efficiency equipment.

This Standard, focusing on new installation requirements, assumes that HVAC equipment and components are in new, factory clean condition. However, if the HVAC equipment is operated during construction phases, or otherwise allowed to deviate from normal cleanliness and/or maintenance parameters, then the HVAC systems may not perform as expected even when proper installation procedures are observed. In these instances, it may first be necessary to perform system maintenance, or to restore the equipment cleanliness and condition before functional testing and verification is undertaken. Users of this Standard are encouraged to review the references in Appendix E pertaining to HVAC system maintenance and cleaning.

This Standard details a level of performance that, if satisfactorily achieved, serves as an indicator that sound industry practices were followed during the design and equipment installation phases. Users of this document are advised to consider additional good practices not provided in the body of this Standard. An illustrative list of additional important good practices and considerations is presented in informative Appendix A. For reference, informative Appendix B contains the under- and over-sizing limits extracted from ANSI/ACCA 3 Manual S – 2014. Informative Appendix C identifies business practices that contractors may find advantageous in positioning themselves to deliver quality installations on a consistent basis in the field. For convenience to the user, informative Appendix D contains generally-accepted industry definitions for a number of terms and acronyms used within the Standard. Finally, informative Appendix E highlights other references that may aid in the design, installation, servicing, maintenance, and cleaning of HVAC systems. Program Administrators and Program Participants are encouraged to also review ANSI/ACCA 9 QIvp (*HVAC Quality Installation Verification Protocols*). The QIvp Standard establishes minimum requirements for verifying that residential and light commercial HVAC systems meet the requirements of this QI Standard.

TABLE OF CONTENTS

Acknowledgements i

Foreword v

Introduction vi

1.0   PURPOSE 1

2.0   SCOPE 1
        2.1   Equipment Types 1
        2.2   Equipment Systems / Components 1

3.0   DESIGN ASPECTS 2
        3.1   Ventilation 2
        3.2   Building Heat Gain / Loss Load Calculations 2
        3.3   Proper Equipment Capacity Selection 3
        3.4   Geothermal Heat Pump Ground Heat Exchanger 4
        3.5   Matched Systems 5

4.0   EQUIPMENT INSTALLATION ASPECTS 6
        4.1   Airflow Through Indoor Heat Exchangers 6
        4.2   Water Flow Through Indoor Heat Exchangers 7
        4.3   Refrigerant Charge 8
        4.4   Electrical Requirements 9
        4.5   On-Rate for Fuel-Fired Equipment 10
        4.6   Combustion Venting System 11
        4.7   System Controls 12

5.0   DISTRIBUTION ASPECTS 14
        5.1   Duct Leakage 14
        5.2   Airflow Balance 15
        5.3   Hydronic Balance 16

6.0   SYSTEM DOCUMENTATION AND OWNER EDUCATION ASPECTS 18
        6.1   Proper System Documentation to the Owner 18
        6.2   Owner/Operator Education 19

Appendix A | Additional Elements for Quality Installations 26

Appendix B | Equipment Sizing Limits 28

Appendix C | Quality Assured Contractor Elements 29

Appendix D | Definitions 34

Appendix E | Pertinent HVAC Bibliography & Resources 39

1.0 PURPOSE

This Standard details the nationally-recognized minimum criteria for the proper installation of HVAC systems in residential and commercial applications.

2.0 SCOPE

This Standard applies to HVAC equipment/components being installed in new and existing residential and commercial buildings:

2.1 EQUIPMENT TYPES

2.1.1 Unitary air conditioners, air-source/water-source heat pumps, and geothermal heat pumps,

2.1.2 Furnaces (gas-fired, oil-fired, electric, and other),

2.1.3 Boilers (gas-fired, oil-fired, electric, and other).

EXCEPTIONS:
Due to differing design aspects and control/operation situations, built-up systems (i.e., chillers, custom or specialty-built penthouse units, etc.) are not included in this Standard. Buildings employing built-up systems are generally designed by architects or professional engineers. Additionally, commercial buildings using built-up equipment are more likely to benefit from increased owner scrutiny via building commissioners, owner agents, etc.

2.2 EQUIPMENT SYSTEMS / COMPONENTS

2.2.1 <u>Heating Systems / Components – Single-zone and Multi-zone</u>
   a) Heating-only equipment and heat pumps including air-source, water-source, and geothermal heat pumps;
   b) Hot-water coil and/or fin-tube radiation, and/or unit heaters, and/or unit ventilators;
   c) Electric resistance coil and/or fin-tube radiation, and/or gas unit heaters, and/or unit ventilators;
   d) Hot air heating (fossil fuel or electric furnace, direct-fired and indirect-fired makeup air equipment);
   e) Radiant heat equipment.

2.2.2 <u>Cooling Systems / Components – Single-zone and Multi-zone</u>
   a) Cooling-only equipment and heat pumps including air-source, water-source, and geothermal heat pumps;
   b) Rooftop single-zone, rooftop multi-zone (hot-deck/cold-deck);
   c) Single-zone unitary (packaged terminal air conditioners/heat pumps, split-coil-ductless).

3.0 DESIGN ASPECTS

This Section focuses on the upfront design procedures/tasks[1] undertaken before the equipment is actually installed.

3.1 VENTILATION

> The contractor shall ensure that ventilation calculations are performed for HVAC system installations/replacements.

3.1.1 REQUIREMENTS

The contractor shall ensure building ventilation requirements (outside air, exhaust air, and building pressurization) are performed to recognized standards, codes, or requirements per authority having jurisdiction (AHJ).[2]

3.1.2 ACCEPTABLE PROCEDURES

The contractor shall follow an appropriate methodology (e.g., ASHRAE 62.1 and 62.2) to perform building ventilation calculations.

3.1.3 ACCEPTABLE DOCUMENTATION

The contractor shall include documentation in the installation file indicating that the ventilation calculations were addressed.[3]

3.2 BUILDING HEAT GAIN / LOSS LOAD CALCULATIONS

> The contractor shall ensure that heat loss and heat gain load calculations are performed for HVAC system installations/replacements.

3.2.1 REQUIREMENTS

The contractor shall ensure:

a) For NEW CONSTRUCTION, or with modification of the existing duct system or hydronic piping system, room-by-room heat gain/loss load calculations are completed,
   or

---

[1] Informative Note: During the HVAC system design process, duct sizing calculations need be undertaken to meet the requirements of ACCA 1 Manual D – 2014, or ACCA Manual Q, and comply with codes to satisfy QI requirements:
– §4.1 & §4.2 Airflow & water flow Across Indoor Heat Exchangers
– §5.2 Airflow Balance

[2] Mechanical ventilation connected to the HVAC system shall not allow the entering mixed-air temperature to be outside the temperature and humidity limits of the OEM heating and air conditioning equipment requirements.

[3] The ventilation load is to be included in the overall heat gain/loss load calculations (§3.2)

b) For EXISTING CONSTRUCTION, without modification of the existing duct system or hydronic piping system, block load heat gain/loss load calculations are completed.

NOTE 1. EXISTING BUILDING EXCEPTION:
Building heat gain / loss load calculations are not required if the original load calculations are on hand and accurately reflect the building's current construction and use.

NOTE 2. LOAD CALCULATIONS:
Room-by-room load calculations may be undertaken if so chosen by the contractor.

3.2.2 ACCEPTABLE PROCEDURES

The contractor shall perform one of the following acceptable procedures for fulfilling the desired criteria:

a) Follow an appropriate methodology/procedure to perform building load calculations per ACCA Manual J®, ACCA Manual N®, or other approved equivalents per the AHJ[4],
or

b) Confirm that the calculations were performed by a qualified third party per the requirements of 3.2.2.a above.

3.2.3 ACCEPTABLE DOCUMENTATION

The contractor shall provide evidence of the following:

a) Form J1 or N1, and Worksheets A included in the installation file,
or

b) Equivalent load calculation documentation in the installation file.

3.3 PROPER EQUIPMENT CAPACITY SELECTION

> The contractor shall ensure that equipment is properly sized and selected prior to being installed.

3.3.1 REQUIREMENTS

The contractor shall ensure the selected equipment satisfies the building's load requirements at the design conditions, and that the equipment capacity (at the design conditions) falls within the minimum and maximum sizing limits specified in recognized industry standards.

3.3.2 ACCEPTABLE PROCEDURES

The contractor shall use OEM performance information and shall adhere to one of the following for capacity limits:

a) For RESIDENTIAL APPLICATIONS, ACCA Manual S,

or

---

[4] Visit www.acca.org/standards/software for a list of ACCA approved software.

b) For COMMERCIAL APPLICATIONS, ACCA Manual CS, OEM guidelines, OEM equipment selection programs, or other approved equivalent per the AHJ.

NOTE. SIZING LIMITS TABLE:
For convenience to the user, informative Appendix B (Equipment Sizing Limits) references under- and over-sizing limits contained within ANSI/ACCA 3 Manual S – 2014.

3.3.3 ACCEPTABLE DOCUMENTATION

The contractor shall provide evidence of the following:

a) Equipment performance information/calculations for the design conditions in the-installation file,
and
b) Written job documentation or checklist in installation file.

3.4 GEOTHERMAL HEAT PUMP GROUND HEAT EXCHANGER

> The contractor shall observe industry-recognized design practices for the proper design of the exterior ground heat exchanger.

3.4.1 REQUIREMENTS

The contractor shall ensure ground heat exchangers are designed to satisfy the HEATING AND COOLING load requirements of the building.

i. The ground interface heat exchanger fluid[5] temperatures [extremes] and flow rates used as the basis for design equipment capacity are within the range specified in OEM guidelines,
and
ii. The ground heat exchange design methodology incorporates:
- building loads and total installed equipment capacity,
- ground heat exchanger type, materials, and geometry,
- soil thermal characteristics,
- climatic characteristics of the project location.

3.4.2 ACCEPTABLE PROCEDURES

The contractor shall follow OEM guidance, recognized industry practices (ASHRAE, IGSHPA, NGWA), or procedures approved by the AHJ.

3.4.3 ACCEPTABLE DOCUMENTATION

The contractor shall include documentation in the installation file indicating that the ground heat exchanger design objectives were met using OEM, IGSHPA, NGWA, ASHRAE, or procedures approved by the AHJ.

---

[5] Fluids may be water- or antifreeze solution for closed loop ground heat exchangers - or refrigerants in DX-based ground heat exchangers. Verify fluid is allowed by local ground water authority or administrative authority.

3.5 MATCHED SYSTEMS

> The contractor shall ensure that heating and cooling equipment are properly matched systems as identified by industry-recognized certification programs.

3.5.1 REQUIREMENTS

The contractor shall ensure that the indoor and outdoor equipment are properly matched.

3.5.2 ACCEPTABLE PROCEDURES

The contractor shall use one of the following acceptable procedures for fulfilling the desired criteria:

a) Confirmation of system matching compliance as compared to a recognized product certification database (AHRI Product Certification directory/database or CEE directory of AHRI-verified equipment),
   or
b) Confirmation of the matched system operational performance data to OEM documentation for all equipment being installed (i.e., air handling unit, indoor coil, outdoor condensing unit),
   or
c) OEM certification letter specific to the equipment as designed and installed.

3.5.3 ACCEPTABLE DOCUMENTATION

The contractor shall provide evidence of the following:

a) Copy of the AHRI *or* CEE-AHRI record/certificate, with appropriate reference number indicated for the matched system, in the installation file,
   or
b) Copy of OEM-provided catalog data, indicating acceptable combination selection and performance data, in the installation file,
   or
c) Copy of OEM-provided letter indicating acceptable combination selection and performance data (e.g. latent and sensible cooling capacity, heating capacity, SEER, EER, HSPF, as applicable) with model numbers in the installation file.

4.0 EQUIPMENT INSTALLATION ASPECTS

This Section focuses on the HVAC system installation.

4.1 AIRFLOW THROUGH INDOOR HEAT EXCHANGERS

> The contractor shall verify that the airflow through the indoor blower unit, (e.g. furnace, fan coil, air handler) is within acceptable CFM ranges.

4.1.1 REQUIREMENTS

The contractor shall ensure measured airflow[6] through the indoor heat exchanger (with all accessories and system components in place).

a) For cooling (e.g., refrigerant, water) and heat pump applications:
   i. Airflow at fan speed setting specified by the design is within 15% of the design airflow,
   and
   ii. Airflow through the unit is within the CFM range listed in the OEM product data,[7]
   and
   iii. Measured external static pressure (ESP)[8] is:
      1) Within OEM-specified acceptable range,
      and
      2) Not more than 25% or 0.10 IWC (whichever is greater) over the calculated ESP used to design the duct system. [Exception for existing buildings: comparing measured ESP to a design ESP is not required for change-out applications, if there has been no modification to the pre-existing ductwork as there is no design ESP.]

b) For gas-fired, oil-fired, or electric heat exchanger applications:
   i. Airflow through the heat exchanger is within 15% of the design airflow,
   and
   ii. Airflow through the indoor heat exchanger is within the CFM range listed in the OEM product data,
   and
   iii. Heat exchanger airflow requirements shall be considered separately for each combined and attached cooling coil sharing the same distribution duct system,
   and
   iv. Measured external static pressure (ESP) is:
      1) Within OEM-specified acceptable range,
      and
      2) Not more than 25% or 0.10 IWC (whichever is greater) over the calculated ESP used to design the duct system. [Exception for

---

[6] When verifying design airflow at design fan speed, there is little distinction between a split capacitor fan motor (PSC), or a variable-speed fan motor (e.g., brushless DC, electronically commutated motor, ECM). See "Airflow" in Appendix D. Note: ECM fan motors are designed to modify their RPMs in order to provide a prescribed (programmed) air volume in response to static pressure conditions (actually torque on the output shaft). Hence, an ECM may use more or less power than a comparable PSC motor in the same application.

[7] Airflow across the coil is typically between 350 to 450 CFM per ton. Adjustments may be needed between dry and wet coils.

[8] Static pressure measurements require clean components: filters, coils, and fans for each indoor unit type.

existing buildings: comparing measured ESP to a design ESP is not required for change-out applications if there has been no modification to the pre-existing ductwork as there is no design ESP.]

NOTE. DUCT LEAKAGE AND AIRFLOW BALANCE:
If duct sealing (§5.1) operations are undertaken, or airflow balance (§5.2) adjustments are made, then the requirements of this section are to be re-performed and recorded on updated documentation.

4.1.2 ACCEPTABLE PROCEDURES

The contractor shall use one of the following acceptable methods for fulfilling the design criteria:

a) OEM CFM/ESP table method using an air differential meter (e.g., manometer) to determine the static pressure drop across a cooling coil, furnace, or fan coil unit, and compare with OEM values (use OEM wet/dry coil information as applicable),
or

b) Traversing using a manometer and probe or an anemometer per ACCA, AABC, ASHRAE, ASTM, NEBB, SMACNA, or TABB procedures,
or

c) Flow grid measurement method,
or

d) Pressure matching method[9],
or

e) The temperature rise method (for heating only at steady-state condition; gas or oil furnace, electric resistance heat, geothermal and water source heat pump) to verify proper airflow through the heat exchanger or heater elements. [NOTE: It is not acceptable to use the temperature rise method to determine cooling airflow over the indoor coil.]

4.1.3 ACCEPTABLE DOCUMENTATION

The contractor shall provide evidence of the following:

a) Documented field data and calculations recorded on start-up sheet,
or

b) Documented field data and calculations recorded on service records,
and

c) Written job documentation or checklist in the installation file.

4.2 WATER FLOW THROUGH INDOOR HEAT EXCHANGERS

The contractor shall verify that the water flow[10] through the refrigerant-to-water, water-to-water, or water-to-air heat exchanger is within acceptable ranges.

4.2.1 REQUIREMENTS

The contractor shall ensure:

---

[9] Use of a calibrated fan to match the supply plenum pressure and measurement of the system airflow through the active fan. Note: Methods for use with brushless DC or ECM blowers in accordance with the motor or OEM instructions.

[10] Water may be treated, or contain antifreeze.

a) Water flow through the heat exchanger is within 10% of the water flow required per the system design,
and
b) Water flow through the heat exchanger is within the range listed in the OEM product data.

4.2.2 ACCEPTABLE PROCEDURES

The contractor shall test using one of the following acceptable methods for fulfilling the desired criteria:
a) The water pressure drop method,
or
b) The water temperature change method,
or
c) Any method approved and specifically stated by the OEM that can be used to determine the water flow rate.

4.2.3 ACCEPTABLE DOCUMENTATION

The contractor shall provide evidence of the following:

a) Documented field data and calculations recorded on start-up sheet,
or
b) Documented field data and calculations recorded on service records,
and
c) Written job documentation or checklist in the installation file.

4.3 REFRIGERANT CHARGE

> The contractor shall ensure that the HVAC system has the proper refrigerant charge.

4.3.1 REQUIREMENTS

The contractor shall ensure:

a) For the SUPERHEAT method, system refrigerant charging per OEM data/instructions and within ± 5°F of the OEM-specified superheat value,
or
b) For the SUBCOOLING method, system refrigerant charging per OEM data/instructions and within ± 3°F of the OEM-specified subcooling value,
or
c) Any method approved and specifically stated by the OEM that will ensure proper refrigerant charging of the system.

NOTE 1. FLOW THROUGH THE HEAT EXCHANGER:
Proper airflows (§4.1) and/or water flows (§4.2) through the heat exchanger must be within acceptable OEM tolerances before the refrigerant charge can be measured and/or adjusted.

NOTE 2. MEASUREMENT PARAMETERS:
The system must be within the OEM's temperature parameters at steady-state conditions before system charge measurements are undertaken.

NOTE 3. REFRIGERANT CHARGE TOLERANCES:
Refrigerant charge tolerances noted (i.e., ± 5°F and/or ± 3°F of the OEM-recommended optimal refrigerant charge for superheat or subcooling, respectively) are not additive to any OEM-specified tolerances.

4.3.2 ACCEPTABLE PROCEDURES

The contractor shall use one of the following acceptable procedures for completing the desired measurements after confirmation of required airflow (per §4.1) and/or water flow (per §4.2) through the indoor coil:

a) Superheat test done under outdoor ambient conditions, as specified by the OEM instructions (typically, 55°F drybulb temperature or higher),
   or
b) Subcooling test done under outdoor ambient conditions, as specified by the OEM instructions (typically, 60°F or higher),
   or
c) Any method approved and specifically documented by the OEM that will ensure proper refrigerant charging of the system.

NOTE: If outdoor conditions require a follow-up visit to finalize the charging process, this should be recorded at both the initial visit and the follow-up visit.

4.3.3 ACCEPTABLE DOCUMENTATION

The contractor shall provide evidence of the following:

a) Documented field data AND operating conditions recorded on start-up sheet,
   or
b) Documented field data AND operating conditions recorded on service records,
   and
c) Written job documentation or checklist in the installation file.

4.4 ELECTRICAL REQUIREMENTS

> The contractor shall ensure electrical requirements are met as related to the installed equipment.

4.4.1 REQUIREMENTS

The contractor shall ensure:

a) LINE and LOW VOLTAGES are per equipment (single- and three-phase) rating nameplate - the percentage (or amount) below or above nameplate values are within OEM specifications and/or code requirements,
   and
b) AMPERAGES are per equipment (single- and three-phase) rating nameplate - the percentage (or amount) below or above nameplate values are within OEM specifications and/or code requirements,
   and
c) LINE and LOW-VOLTAGE wiring sizes per NEC (National Electric Code), or equivalent,
   and
d) GROUNDING/BONDING per NEC, or equivalent.

4.4.2 ACCEPTABLE PROCEDURES

The contractor shall test using the following acceptable procedures for fulfilling the design criteria:

a) Volt meter to measure the voltage,
   and
b) Ammeter to measure the amperage,
   and
c) Verify measurements with nameplate and over-current protection criteria.

4.4.3 ACCEPTABLE DOCUMENTATION

The contractor shall provide evidence of the following:

a) Documents showing that selections are in compliance with OEM specifications,
   and
b) Written job documentation or checklist in the installation file.

4.5 ON-RATE FOR FUEL-FIRED EQUIPMENT

> The contractor shall ensure the equipment combustion is "on-rate", for gas-fired or oil-fired equipment, and is at the equipment nameplate value.

4.5.1 REQUIREMENTS

The contractor shall ensure:

a) Gas-Fired Equipment:

   The contractor shall ensure:
   i. Firing rate within ± 5% of nameplate input for gas equipment (or per OEM specifications),
      and
   ii. Temperature rise within the nameplate limits.

b) Oil-Fired Equipment:

   The contractor shall ensure:
   i. Correct nozzle gph and spray angle were installed,
      and
   ii. Correct oil pump pressure for nozzle installed and at OEM's specified values,
      and
   iii. Temperature rise per nameplate limits.

4.5.2 ACCEPTABLE PROCEDURES

a) Gas-Fired Equipment:

   The contractor shall test using one of the following acceptable procedures for fulfilling the desired criteria:
   i. Perform a combustion analysis per OEM installation or gas burner instructions,
      or

ii. Clocking the meter or other fuel input measurement per OEM instruction *and* measuring the temperature rise at steady-state conditions (with airflow first verified by §4.1) – furnaces only.

b) Oil-Fired Equipment:

The contractor shall fulfill the following criteria:
i. Perform a combustion analysis per OEM installation and oil burner instructions[11],
and
ii. Verify nozzle or alternate input nozzle per OEM installation and oil burner instructions, *and* verify oil pump pressure with a dial or electronic gauge designed for oil pressure measurement, *and* measure the temperature rise at steady-state conditions (with airflow first verified by §4.1) – furnaces only.

4.5.3 ACCEPTABLE DOCUMENTATION

The contractor shall provide evidence of the following:

a) Documented field data recorded on start-up sheet,
and
b) Written job documentation or checklist in the installation file.

4.6 COMBUSTION VENTING SYSTEM

> The contractor shall ensure proper sizing, design, material selection and assembly of the combustion gas venting system.

4.6.1 REQUIREMENTS

The contractor shall install the vent system to:

a) CATEGORY I vent system sized per OEM instructions and the National Fuel Gas Code (NFGC, NFPA 54) for gas-fired appliances, or OEM instructions and NFPA 31 for oil-fired appliances,
or
b) CATEGORY I vent system sized per OEM instructions and the International Fuel Gas Code (IFGC),
or
c) CATEGORY I vent system sized per OEM instructions and the Uniform Mechanical Code (UMC),
or
d) CATEGORY II, III and IV vent system sized per OEM instructions,
and
e) CATEGORY II, III and IV vent system sized per the AHJ.

4.6.2 ACCEPTABLE PROCEDURES

The contractor shall use one of the following acceptable procedures for fulfilling the installation criteria:

---

[11] Combustion analysis is necessary when setting up an oil burner. Additionally, new oil-fired equipment no longer standardizes the pump pressure at 100 psig. Hence, incorrect pump pressure may result in an incorrect input rate for the equipment.

a) Comparison of the actual installation to appropriate fuel gas venting tables for Category I vent systems,
   or
   b) Comparison of the actual installation to appropriate OEM instructions, and local codes for Category II, III and IV vent systems.

4.6.3 ACCEPTABLE DOCUMENTATION

The contractor shall provide evidence of the following:

   a) Documented field data recorded on start-up sheet,
   or
   b) Documented field data recorded on service records,
   and
   c) Written job documentation or checklist in the installation file.

4.7 SYSTEM CONTROLS

> The contractor shall ensure proper selection and functioning of system operational and safety controls.

4.7.1 REQUIREMENTS

The contractor shall ensure:

   a) Operating controls and safety controls are compatible with the system type and application, and the selected controls are consistent with OEM recommendations and industry practices,
   and
   b) Operating controls and safety controls lead to proper sequencing of equipment functions, with all controls and safeties functioning per OEM,
   and
   c) Operating controls and safety controls for field-installed components shall function per OEM specifications.

   NOTE. OPERATING CONTROLS:
   Examples of operating controls include: thermostats, humidistats, economizer controls, hydronic outdoor reset controls, etc. Examples of safety controls include: temperature limit switch, airflow switch, condensate overflow switch, furnace limit switch, boiler limit switch, etc.

4.7.2 ACCEPTABLE PROCEDURES

The contractor shall use the following acceptable procedures for fulfilling the desired design criteria:

   a) Confirmation of the control/safety selections made,
   and
   b) Supporting OEM literature related to the selections made,
   and
   c) Verification of correct cycling/operational sequences of controls and safety devices/systems per system design and OEM specifications.

4.7.3 ACCEPTABLE DOCUMENTATION

The contractor shall provide evidence of the following:

a) Documents showing that field-installed controls/safeties selections are in compliance with OEM specifications,
   and
b) Written job documentation or checklist in the installation file indicating that field-installed controls/safeties function properly.

5.0 DISTRIBUTION ASPECTS

This Section focuses on heating and cooling delivery elements of the installed HVAC system.

5.1 DUCT LEAKAGE

> The contractor shall ensure the ducts are sealed and that air leakage (CFM) is minimized.

5.1.1 REQUIREMENTS

The contractor shall ensure:

a) For NEW CONSTRUCTION, test using any one of the three options:
   i. Ducts (100%) located inside the thermal envelope have no more than 10% total duct leakage (airflow in CFM),
   or
   ii. Ducts (any portion) located outside the thermal envelope have no more than 6% total duct leakage (airflow in CFM),
   or
   iii. Per local code or the AHJ.

b) For EXISTING CONSTRUCTION, test using any one of the three options:
   i. No more than 20% total duct leakage (airflow in CFM),
   or
   ii. 50% improvement on existing leakage rate, or until 5.1.1.b.i. is achieved,
   or
   iii. Per local code or the AHJ.

NOTE 1. DUCT LEAKAGE:
The total duct leakage allowable pertains to the percentage of CFM leakage as compared to the overall air handling fan flow (see §4.1) operating at design conditions. The airflow leakage allowable shall be based on the higher of the winter heating airflow, or of the summer cooling airflow.
TOTAL duct leakage = SUPPLY duct leakage + RETURN duct leakage.

NOTE 2. DUCT SEALING:
For duct sealing, all duct sealing materials shall be listed and labeled to UL 181A or UL 181B specifications and shall be used in strict accordance with OEM instructions.

NOTE 3. AIRFLOW AND ESP:
If duct sealing operations are undertaken, the requirements in §4.1 (airflow through the heat exchanger and measured ESP) are to be re-performed and recorded on updated documentation.

5.1.2 ACCEPTABLE PROCEDURES

The contractor shall test using one of the following acceptable procedures for fulfilling the desired criteria:

a) Duct pressurization tests[12] at 25 Pascal,

---

[12] Duct leakage is measured using a duct pressurization test through a calibrated fan or orifice. Duct registers are sealed, a fan is attached to one opening, the ducts are pressurized, and the amount of air flowing through the fan is quantified.

or

    b) For EXISTING CONSTRUCTION, airflow comparison method[13],
    or
    c) ANSI/SMACNA Air Duct Leakage Test Manual,
    or
    d) Duct pressurization test at referenced pressure standard by the AHJ.

5.1.3 ACCEPTABLE DOCUMENTATION

The contractor shall provide evidence of the following:

    a) Documented field data recorded on start-up sheet,
    or
    b) Documented field data recorded on service records,
    and
    c) Written job documentation or checklist in the installation file.

5.2 AIRFLOW BALANCE

> The contractor shall ensure room and ventilation airflows meet the design/application requirements.

5.2.1. REQUIREMENTS

The contractor shall ensure:

    a) For NEW CONSTRUCTION or addition of new ducts to an existing structure (with interior doors closed AND open) –
        For Residential Buildings: The individual room airflows are within the greater of ± 20%, or 25 CFM of the design/application requirements for the supply and return ducts.
        For Commercial Buildings: The individual room airflows are within the greater of ± 10%, or 25 CFM of the design/application requirements for the supply and return ducts.
    or
    For EXISTING CONSTRUCTION without contractor modification of existing ductwork: No additional ACCA QI requirements apply.
    or
    For NEW OR EXISTING CONSTRUCTION the airflow balance is per local code or the AHJ.
    and
    b) For ventilation air added to NEW OR EXISTING CONSTRUCTION, ventilation airflow will be within the greater of ± 20%, or ± 15 CFM of the design/application requirements.

NOTE. AIRFLOW THROUGH INDOOR HEAT EXCHANGERS:
Per §4.1, airflow through the heat exchanger must be within the OEM's specified range for all furnace, fan coil, and air handler applications.

---

[13] Total room supply CFMs and return CFMs compared with blower capability, as per procedures specified by ACCA, AABC, NEBB and TABB. Active / powered equipment recommended over passive equipment.

5.2.2 ACCEPTABLE PROCEDURES

The contractor shall test using one of the following acceptable devices for fulfilling the desired criteria:

a) Airflow measuring device (AMD) used per specifications from the AMD manufacturer,
or
b) Duct traverse with Pitot tube and manometer per procedures specified by ACCA, AABC, ASHRAE, NEBB, SMACNA or TABB,
or
c) Measure the average airflow using an anemometer (hotwire or rotary) per specifications from the test equipment manufacturer.[14]

5.2.3 ACCEPTABLE DOCUMENTATION

The contractor shall provide evidence of the following:

a) Documented field data recorded on start-up sheet or test and balance form,
or
b) Documented field data recorded on service records,
and
c) Written job documentation or checklist in the installation file.

5.3 HYDRONIC BALANCE

> The contractor shall ensure water flows meet the design/application requirements.

5.3.1. REQUIREMENTS

The contractor shall ensure:

a) For NEW CONSTRUCTION, or addition of new piping to an existing HVAC system, the water flow to individual room or zone heat exchangers are within ± 10% of the design/application GPM requirements.
or
b) For EXISTING CONSTRUCTION without contractor modification of existing piping: No additional ACCA QI requirements apply.
or
c) For NEW OR EXISTING CONSTRUCTION the room/zone hydronic balance is per local code or authority having jurisdiction.

NOTE. WATER FLOW THROUGH HEAT EXCHANGER:
Per §4.2, water flow through the heat exchanger must be within the OEM's specified range for all boilers, and water-to-water geothermal heat pump applications.

---

[14] The use of anemometers is acceptable if (1) grille "free areas" are known and if (2) the measurement tolerances for the instrument/device being used are considerable tighter than the airflow balance tolerances. The grill "free area" is commonly known as the area-K (or Ak), and the values are provided by the grille/diffuser OEM.

5.3.2 ACCEPTABLE PROCEDURES

The contractor shall use one of the following acceptable tests for fulfilling the desired criteria:

a) Manometer and probe used per instructions from the instrument manufacturer,
   or
b) Ultrasonic/Doppler flow meter used per instructions from the instrument manufacturer,
   or
c) Pressure gauge used per instructions from the instrument manufacturer,
   or
d) Procedures specified by OEM.

5.3.3 ACCEPTABLE DOCUMENTATION

The contractor shall provide evidence of the following:

a) A copy of documented field data recorded on start-up sheet or test and balance form,
   or
b) Documented field data recorded on service records,
   and
c) Written job documentation or checklist in the installation file.

6.0 SYSTEM DOCUMENTATION AND OWNER EDUCATION ASPECTS

This Section focuses on providing owners with job documentation, operation instructions, and education to assist them in properly operating and maintaining their systems.

6.1 PROPER SYSTEM DOCUMENTATION TO THE OWNER

> The contractor shall provide records pertaining to the HVAC system installation as well as the operation and maintenance to be performed.

6.1.1 REQUIREMENTS

The contractor shall ensure:

a) An installation file of required and relevant information is created and provided to the client, or the building owner/operator, or designated agent.
   i) Required documentation: Information detailed in the *Acceptable Documentation*[15] for each applicable Section of this Standard.
   and
   ii) Relevant documentation: additional information applicable to the HVAC activity undertaken.
   and
b) Copies of documents from §6.1.1.a and a record of the model and serial numbers for all equipment installed are maintained at the contractor's place of business.

6.1.2 ACCEPTABLE PROCEDURES

The contractor shall confirm that all the listed requirements are met.

(See Table 1)

6.1.3 ACCEPTABLE DOCUMENTATION

The contractor shall provide evidence of the following:

a) Written job documentation or checklist in the installation file,
   and
b) Signed documentation from the customer that the listed requirements were offered/met.

---

[15] Examples of required acceptable documentation include: ventilation calculations (§3.1), load calculations (§3.2), OEM performance data (§3.3), ground heat exchanger design (§3.4), AHRI certificates (§3.5), records of measurements (§4.1, §4.2, §4.3, §4.4, §4.5), documented field data (§4.6), written documentation of proper operation sequences (§4.7), duct leakage tests (§5.1), test and balance reports (§5.2, §5.3), and customer education (§6.2).

6.2 OWNER/OPERATOR EDUCATION

> The contractor shall inform the customer on how to both operate and maintain the installed equipment, and will promote system maintenance to aid in the continuing performance of the installed equipment.

6.2.1 REQUIREMENTS

The contractor shall ensure:

a) Customers are instructed on system operation of installed equipment,
   and
b) Customers are instructed on the maintenance requirements for the installed equipment,
   and
c) Customers are instructed on warranty procedures and responsibilities,
   and
d) Customers are provided with contact information for warranty, maintenance, and service requirements.

6.2.2 ACCEPTABLE PROCEDURES

The contractor shall confirm that all the listed requirements are met.

6.2.3 ACCEPTABLE DOCUMENTATION

The contractor shall provide evidence of the following:

a) Written job documentation or checklist in the installation file,
   or
b) Signed documentation from the customer that the listed requirements were offered/met; including the date and names of the trainer and the building owner/operator (or designated agent) receiving the instruction,
   or
c) Documentation that the builder was provided with the training materials.

Table 1 Quality Installation Required Documentation		
QI Standard Element	Approved Procedure	Reported Information
Design Aspects (§3.0 QI Standard) — §3.1 Ventilation	ASHRAE 62.1 or ASHRAE 62.2	✓ Ventilation rate based on building use ✓ Floor area ✓ Number of occupants ✓ Number of bedrooms ✓ Estimated infiltration

§3.2 Load calculation	Manual J or Manual N or AHJ-approved equivalent	✓ Design conditions :
		  ○ Outdoor temps ○ Latitude ○ Indoor temps
		  ○ Grains diff ○ Altitude ○ Infiltration
		  ○ Orientation ○ Occupants ○ Duct load
		✓ Opaque building components (walls, ceilings, etc)
		  ○ Area of component ○ HTM of component
		✓ For windows
		  ○ Area ○ Adjusted HTM
		  ○ Heating U value ○ SHGC
		  ○ Orientation ○ Overhang dimensions
		✓ Calculated loads
		  ○ Total heating ○ Sensible cooling
		  ○ Total cooling ○ Latent cooling

§3.3 & §3.4 Equipment capacity selection	Air Conditioner (from OEM performance data)	✓ Equipment model ✓ Outdoor ambient dry-bulb ✓ Indoor entering wet-bulb ✓ Indoor entering dry-bulb ✓ Airflow across the heat exchanger ✓ Equipment Sensible Capacity ✓ Equipment Latent Capacity
	Heat Pump (from OEM performance data)	✓ Equipment model ✓ Outdoor ambient dry-bulb ✓ Indoor entering wet-bulb ✓ Indoor entering dry-bulb ✓ Airflow across the heat exchanger ✓ Equipment Sensible Capacity ✓ Equipment Latent Capacity
	Geothermal Heat Pump (from OEM performance data)	✓ Equipment model ✓ Outdoor ambient dry-bulb ✓ Indoor entering wet-bulb ✓ Indoor entering dry-bulb ✓ Airflow across the heat exchanger ✓ Design water flow through the equipment ✓ Design ground temperature ✓ Equipment Sensible Capacity ✓ Equipment Latent Capacity
	Furnace (from OEM performance data)	✓ Equipment model ✓ Output Btu/H
	Boiler (from OEM performance data)	✓ Equipment model ✓ Output Btu/H
	Electric Heater (from OEM performance data)	✓ Equipment model ✓ Output Btu/H at: ✓ Rated kW ✓ Volts and amps
§3.5 Matched systems		✓ AHRI Directory Certificate, or ✓ CEE Directory Certificate, or ✓ OEM Catalog Performance Data

Table 1 Quality Installation Required Documentation			
	QI Standard Element	Approved Procedure	Reported Information
Equipment Aspects (§4.0 QI Standard)	§4.1 Airflow through the heat exchanger	OEM/Cfm external/total Static Pressure Drop and/or Coil Table OR	✓ Equipment fan speed setting ✓ Supply side SP ✓ Return side SP ✓ Design airflow ✓ Measured airflow (Fan flow based on measured ESP, voltage, and fan speed)
		Duct system traverse OR	✓ Duct's inside dimensions ✓ Number of readings taken ✓ Average velocity ✓ Are ducts lined or internally insulated? ✓ Location of traverse test site ✓ Design airflow ✓ Measured airflow
		Flow grid measurement OR	✓ Flow grid test site (e.g., unit filter rack, etc) ✓ Altitude adjustment ✓ Air temperature adjustment ✓ Average air velocity ✓ Flow grid area ✓ Design airflow ✓ Measured airflow
		Pressure matching method: Supply air pressure matching OR	✓ Supply duct static pressure, unit fan only ✓ Location of pressure reading ✓ Calibrated fan pressure at supply static pressure ✓ Design airflow ✓ Measured airflow (Calibrated fan flow at corresponding pressure)
		Temperature rise method (**electric** heat only) OR	✓ Measured temperature rise (supply - return air temp) ✓ Measured volts (at electrical disconnect) ✓ Measured amps (at electrical disconnect) ✓ Annotate Single Ø or Three Ø heater ✓ Design airflow ✓ Measured airflow
		Temperature rise method (**gas** heat only) OR	✓ Measured temperature rise (supply air - return air) ✓ Measured manifold pressure ✓ OEM-specified manifold pressure ✓ Measured gas flow (time for one revolution of meter) ✓ Fuel gas heating value (from the gas company) ✓ Steady-state heating efficiency ✓ Design airflow ✓ Measured airflow
		Temperature rise method (**oil** heat only)	✓ Measured temperature rise (supply air - return air) ✓ Nozzle size ✓ Nozzle flow rate ✓ Measured pump pressure ✓ Fuel oil heating value (from the oil company) ✓ Steady-state heating efficiency ✓ Design airflow ✓ Measured airflow

Table 1 Quality Installation Required Documentation

	QI Standard Element	Approved Procedure	Reported Information
Equipment Aspects (§4.0 QI Standard)	§4.2 Water flow through the heat exchanger	Pressure drop method: Pressure at inlet and outlet	✓ Number of heat exchangers ✓ Total water volume measured ✓ Location of pressure drop reading ✓ Water flow inlet and outlet pressure ✓ Design water flow ✓ Measured water flow ✓ Antifreeze correction made? Measured specific gravity.
		OR	
		Water temperature change method	✓ Number of heat exchangers ✓ Airflow through the heat exchanger (e.g.: CFM needs to be verified for temperature rise to be correct) ✓ Location of temperature readings ✓ Design water flow ✓ Measured water flow ✓ Antifreeze correction made? Measured specific gravity.
		OR	
		Other OEM approved Method	✓ OEM directions available? ✓ Number of readings taken ✓ Location of test site ✓ Design water flow ✓ Measured water flow ✓ Other measurements as per OEM requirements
	§4.3 Refrigerant charge	Superheat	✓ Airflow over evaporator coil ✓ Refrigerant type ✓ Suction line pressure (at OEM specified location) ✓ Suction line temperature (at OEM specified location) ✓ Entering air temperature and humidity (at steady-state, about 15 minutes) ✓ Outdoor weather conditions (invalid below 55°F, unless specified by OEM) ✓ Expansion device type ✓ OEM-recommended superheat ✓ Measured superheat
		OR	
		Sub-cooling	✓ Airflow over evaporator coil ✓ Refrigerant type ✓ Liquid line pressure (at OEM-specified location) ✓ Liquid line temperature (at OEM-specified location) ✓ Entering air temperature and humidity (at steady-state, about 15 minutes) ✓ Outdoor weather conditions (invalid below 60°F, unless specified by OEM) ✓ Expansion device type ✓ OEM-recommended sub-cooling ✓ Measured sub-cooling
		OR	
		OEM-specified method	✓ List all applicable measurements taken and provide documentation substantiating this procedure for the HVAC system
	§4.4 Electrical requirements		✓ Measured & nameplate line voltage for each component ✓ Measured and listed control voltage ✓ Measured & nameplate line amperage for each component ✓ Measured and listed control amperage ✓ Ensure the equipment is properly grounded ✓ List line wire size and type ✓ List control wire size and type

Table 1 Quality Installation Required Documentation			
	QI Standard Element	Approved Procedure	Reported Information
Equipment Aspects (§4.0 QI Standard)	§4.5 On-Rate for fuel-fired equipment	Gas-fired equipment (Clocking the meter)	✓ Nameplate heating input ✓ Nameplate temperature rise ✓ Fuel gas heating value (from the gas company) ✓ Measured gas flow rate ✓ Measured temperature rise (supply air - return air)
		Gas-fired equipment (Combustion Analysis)	✓ Measured CO level (at high, medium & low fire) ✓ Fuel pressure at burner (at high, medium & low fire) ✓ Draft above draft hood or barometric pressure (at high, medium & low fire) ✓ Steam pressure or water temperature entering and leaving boiler, steam generator, or process heater ✓ Unit rate if meter is available
		Oil-fired equipment (Nozzle, pump pressure, temperature rise)	✓ Nozzle size and flow rate ✓ Measured temperature rise (supply air - return air) ✓ Nameplate temperature rise
		Oil-fired equipment (Combustion Analysis)	✓ Measured CO level (at high, medium & low fire) ✓ Fuel pressure at burner (at high, medium & low fire) ✓ Draft above draft hood or barometric pressure (at high, medium & low fire) ✓ Steam pressure or water temperature entering and leaving boiler, steam generator, or process heater ✓ Unit rate if meter is available
	§4.6 Combustion venting system	Category I per OEM instructions and NFGC ——— OR ———	✓ Number and venting type (natural or fan assisted) of appliances in the venting system ✓ Number and type of offsets in venting system ✓ Altitude of installation (if de-rated for altitude) ✓ Total vent height (in feet) ✓ Total vent lateral length (in feet)
		Category I per OEM instructions and IFGC Or per OEM and UMC	✓ Number and venting type (natural or fan assisted) of appliances in the venting system ✓ Number and type of offsets in venting system ✓ Altitude of installation (if de-rated for altitude) ✓ Total vent height (in feet) ✓ Total vent lateral length (in feet)
		Category II, III, or IV per OEM instructions ——— OR ———	✓ Attach OEM instructions and list required measurements (typical measurements are similar to those for Category I vent system).
		Category II, III, or IV per local code	✓ Attach local code and list required measurements (typical measurements are similar to those for Category I vent system).
	§4.7 System controls	Equipment controls	✓ Type of HVAC system ✓ Type of control ✓ Sequence of operation tested (heat, cool, fan, re-set controls, etc.)
		Safety controls	✓ Type of safety control (e.g., condensate overflow switch) ✓ Method of test (e.g., lifted float, or filled pan with water) ✓ Result of test (e.g., system stopped, compressor stopped)

Table 1 Quality Installation Required Documentation			
	QI Standard Element	Approved Procedure	Reported Information
Distribution Aspects (§5.0 QI Standard)	§5.1 Duct leakage	Duct pressurization test	✓ Qualitative assessment of outdoor wind conditions ✓ Calibrated fan connection point ✓ Duct pressure with reference to outside ✓ Orifice size and associated pressure table (if orifice is used) ✓ Pressure difference across the orifice (if orifice is used) ✓ Calibrated fan pressure ✓ Calibrated fan flow at reported pressure ✓ Duct leakage tolerance ✓ Measured duct leakage
		OR	
		Airflow Comparison method (Commercial only)	✓ Total measured supply CFM ✓ Total measured return CFM ✓ Airflow across the heat exchanger ✓ Duct leakage tolerance ✓ Measured duct leakage
		OR	
		Duct pressurization test per the authority having jurisdiction	✓ Attach local code and list required measurements (typical measurements are similar to those for other duct pressurization tests).
	§5.2 Airflow balance	Flow hood measurements	✓ Design airflow (for each duct terminal) ✓ Measured airflow (for each duct terminal)
		OR	
		Hot-wire or Rotary anemometer	✓ Terminal devices' air velocity ✓ Report terminal devices' Ak factor ✓ Design airflow (for each duct terminal) ✓ Measured airflow (for each duct terminal)
		OR	
		Pitot tube	✓ Duct's inside dimensions ✓ Number of readings taken ✓ Average velocity ✓ Location of traverse test site ✓ Design airflow (for each duct terminal) ✓ Measured airflow (for each duct terminal)

	Table 1 Quality Installation Required Documentation			
	QI Standard Element	Approved Procedure	Reported Information
Distribution Aspects (§5.0 QI Standard)	§5.3 Hydronic Balance	Manometer and probe	✓ Number of heat exchangers ✓ Total water volume measured ✓ Location of pressure drop reading ✓ Water flow inlet and outlet pressure ✓ Design water flow ✓ Measured water flow ✓ Correction factor for compounds other than water
		OR Ultrasonic/Doppler flow meter	✓ Number of heat exchangers ✓ Total water volume measured ✓ Location of pressure drop reading ✓ Type of pipe and meter data sheets ✓ Design water flow ✓ Measured water flow ✓ Correction factor for compounds other than water
		OR Pressure gauge	✓ Number of heat exchangers ✓ Total water volume measured ✓ Location of pressure drop reading ✓ Water flow inlet and outlet pressure ✓ Design water flow ✓ Measured water flow ✓ Correction factor for compounds other than water
		OR OEM Specified Procedures	✓ OEM directions and related charts ✓ Total water volume measured ✓ Design water flow ✓ Measured water flow
Documentation and Education Aspects (§6.0 QI Standard)	§6.1 System Documentation	Required documentation	✓ Ventilation calculations ✓ Load calculations ✓ OEM performance data ✓ AHRI certificates ✓ Records of measurements ✓ Documented field data ✓ Equipment operation sequences ✓ Duct leakage tests ✓ Test and balance reports ✓ Customer education
		Relevant information	✓ Permits ✓ As-built drawings (including the type, size, and location of all underground heat geothermal heat exchange piping) ✓ Survey data ✓ Equipment submittals, ✓ Maintenance and operating instructions ✓ Equipment/contractor warranties
	§6.2 Customer Education	System operation	✓ Signed documentation from the customer or other written documentation
		Maintenance requirements	✓ Signed documentation from the customer or other written documentation
		Warranty procedures	✓ Signed documentation from the customer or other written documentation
		Contact information	✓ Signed documentation from the customer or other written documentation

APPENDIX A | ADDITIONAL ELEMENTS FOR QUALITY INSTALLATIONS

[This Appendix is not part of the Standard. It is merely informative and does not contain requirements necessary for conformance to the Standard. It has not been processed according to the ANSI requirements for a standard and may contain material that has not been subject to public review or a consensus process. Unresolved objectors on informative material are not offered the right to appeal at ACCA or ANSI.]

This list illustrates elements that are important for achieving quality installations. While some of these items are not part of the core specification, it is acknowledged that quality installations will undoubtedly include/consider these aspects as well.

NO.		ASPECTS	GUIDELINES	CONSIDERATIONS	RECOMMENDATIONS
1	MECHANICAL	Load Parameters	- Design temperatures (OUTDOOR and INDOOR) are according to ACCA Manual J®, ACCA Manual N®, local or state code requirements, documented customer requirements, OR other recognized methodology. - Area of walls, windows, skylights and doors are within ± 10% of architectural plans or actual building. - Selected procedure includes: orientation of windows and glass doors (summer HEAT GAIN only); infiltration-rate; duct loads; internal gains.
2		Equipment Clearances	- Clearances sufficient to enable adequate servicing of the equipment and to enable proper airflow around the outdoor unit (per OEM recommendations, International Mechanical Code, Uniform Mechanical Code, local code). - To provide adequate clearances to combustibles (per OEM specifications/recommendations; National Fuel Gas Code; International Association of Plumbing and Mechanical officials; International Fuel Gas Code; International Mechanical Code; Uniform Mechanical Code, local code).
3		Combustion Analysis	- Carbon monoxide (CO): within OEM specifications. - Oxygen (O_2): within OEM specifications. - Stack Temperature: within OEM specifications. - Draft: within OEM specifications. - For oil systems, a smoke test and over-fire draft test are within OEM specifications.
4		Pump(s) (if applicable)	- Properly sized and selected. - Head pressure and flow (GPM) consistent with IBR Guide 2000.
5	PIPING	Refrigerant Circuit Integrity	- Leak-free circuit: achieved by purging with nitrogen during brazing, conducting a nitrogen pressure test, evacuating (triple), and holding to 500 microns or less. - Contaminant-free circuit: including oil removal and flushing of refrigerant lines when substituting HFC or HFC blends for CFCs and HCFCs.
6		Refrigerant Piping	- Sizing/design/insulation: in accordance with OEM specifications. - Materials: copper refrigerant piping must comply with either ASTM B 280 or ASTM B 88. - Assembly: Mechanical joints are not allowed on piping larger than 7/8" annealed copper; all other joints should be brazed as defined using a nonferrous filler material having a melting point above 1000°F (538°C) but lower than the melting points of the materials being joined together.
7		Condensate Drain / Piping	- Sizing/design: in accordance with OEM specifications and/or local jurisdictional codes. - Materials: in accordance with OEM specifications and/or local jurisdictional codes. - Assembly: in accordance with OEM specifications and/or local jurisdictional codes.

Appendix A | Additional Elements for QI

#	Category	Element	Requirements
8		Fossil Fuel Piping	- Sizing/design / Materials / Assembly: in accordance with the current editions of the National Fuel Gas Code or the International Fuel Gas Code, or Uniform Mechanical Code. - Assembly: leak free - check for leakage using approved procedure identified in the current edition of the National Fuel Gas Code, International Fuel Gas Code, or Uniform Mechanical Code. - Appliance gas inlet connections are to remain sealed or capped until final gas piping is connected to the appliance.
9	DISTRIBUTION	Duct Conduction Losses/Gains	- For the installed system (at design conditions), the temperature difference between the temperature at each/any supply register and the temperature at the evaporator coil is less than 5°F, and less than 15°F from the temperature of the heat exchanger or heating element.
10		External Static Pressure Capability	- The duct system should be sized to handle the required system design CFM at the rated static pressure capability of the equipment fan/blower.
11		Air Filtration	- Filters of correct size/selection for equipment application (per application requirement/OEM specifications). - Filter housing is tight with gasketed access panels/doors.
12		Duct Design	- Duct Supply and Duct Return are designed per ACCA Manual D®, ACCA Manual Q®, ASHRAE standards, or per other acceptable engineering methods.
13		Duct Construction	- Duct material selection, construction, assembly and installation are per duct material manufacturer specifications, SMACNA standards, or the authority having jurisdiction. - Flexible ducts and flexible duct connectors shall meet code requirements.
14		Registers, Grilles, Diffusers	- Selection (based on throw, volume, mixing, direction, location) is per ACCA Manual D®, ACCA Manual T®, SMACNA, grill / register / diffuser manufacturer specifications.
15		Rate of Airflow	- Velocity in the duct (FPM) per ACCA Manual D® or approved equal. - Velocity at the grille (FPM) per recommended FPM for the selected grille.
16		Noise	- Decibel (dB) noise levels are compliant with recommendations from the Air Movement and Control Association (AMCA).
17		Sound Reduction	- Isolation for suspended equipment, air handlers, furnaces in attics. - Isolation for roof-mounted or ground-mounted equipment.
18	HYDRONICS	Geothermal	- Sizing and design, piping, materials and joining methods, purging, air elimination, and charging (non-refrigerant), instructions for geothermal heat exchangers must be done in accordance with OEM instructions and applicable ACCA, ASHRAE, AHRI, IGSHPA, and NGWA standards and guidelines.
19		Hydronic Heating Water/Steam Flow	- GPM or lbs/hour - per OEM specifications and system requirements.
20		Hydronic Loop	- Open Loop Systems: Water analysis; verify water quality and quantity meets OEM specifications. - Direct Exchange Ground Source Heat Pump: The copper loop should be protected (corrosion protection system) from corrosion in acidic soil through the use of an anode, or other cathodic protection that meets OEM specifications. - A make-up water analysis should be taken initially of each installation so that the correct water treatment can be established and installed per OEM recommendations.

APPENDIX B | EQUIPMENT SIZING LIMITS

[This Appendix is not part of the Standard. It is merely informative and does not contain requirements necessary for conformance to the Standard. It has not been processed according to the ANSI requirements for a standard and may contain material that has not been subject to public review or a consensus process. Unresolved objectors on informative material are not offered the right to appeal at ACCA or ANSI.]

Overview of Size Limits for Residential HVAC Equipment

Equipment [a] Tested and Rated by the AHRI	Attributes of Local Climate Notes b, c	Issue	Minimum (deficient) and Maximum (excessive) Capacity Factors. [d]					
		Cooling Capacity (Btuh)	Single-Speed Compressor			Multi- and Variable-Speed Compressor		
			Air-Air	GLHP [e]	GWHP [f]	Air-Air	GLHP [e]	GWHP [f]
Air-Air and Water-Air Cooling-Only & Heat Pump	Mild Winter or Has a Latent Cooling Load	Total	0.90 to 1.15		1.25	0.90 to 1.20_{multi} or $1.30_{variable}$		1.30_m or 1.35_v
		Latent	Minimum = 1.00. Preferred maximum = 1.50 (may exceed 1.5 if no reasonable alternative).					
		Sensible	Minimum = 0.90. Maximum determined by total and latent capacities.					
Air-Air and Water-Air Heat Pump Only	Cold Winter and No Latent Cooling load	Total	Maximum capacity = **Manual J** total cooling load plus 15,000 Btuh; Minimum factor = 0.90					
		Latent	Latent capacity for summer cooling is not an issue.					
		Sensible	Not an issue (determined by the limits for total cooling capacity).					

a) Central ducted; ductless single-split; ductless multi-split equipment. AHRI: Air Conditioning, Heating and Refrigeration Institute.
b) Mild winter: Heating degree days for base 65°F divided by cooling degree days for base 50°F less than 2.0. Cold winter = 2.0 or more.
c) Latent cooling load: **Manual J** sensible load divided by **Manual J** total load less than 0.95. No latent load = 0.95 or more.
d) Minimum and maximum capacity factors operate on the total, latent, and sensible capacity values produced by an accurate **Manual J** load calculation (per Section 2 of the Eighth Edition of **Manual J**, version 2.0 or later). Multiply a size factor by 100 to convert to a percentage. For example, 1.15 excess capacity = 115% excess capacity.
e) GLHP: Ground loop heat pump (water in buried closed pipe loop).
f) GWHP: Ground water heat pump (ground water from well, pond, lake, river, etc., flows though equipment and is discarded).

Electric Heating Coils	Furnaces; Heat Pump supplement; emergency	Load (Btuh)	Maximum KW	Minimum Capacity Factor	Maximum Capacity Factor
		≤ 15,000	5.0	Satisfy Load	See Maximum KW
		> 15,000	See Min and Max	0.95	1.75

Minimum and maximum capacity factors operate on the heating load produced by an accurate **Manual J** load calculation. Multiply a size factor by 100 to convert to a percentage.

Natural Gas, Oil, Propane Furnaces	Duty	Minimum Output Capacity	Maximum Output Capacity
	Heating-only	1.00	1.40
	Heating-Cooling Preferred		1.40
	Heating-Cooling Allowed		2.00

Minimum and maximum capacity factors operate on the heating load produced by an accurate **Manual J** load calculation. Multiply a size factor by 100 to convert to a percentage. For heating-cooling duty, blower performance must be compatible with the cooling equipment.

Electric, and Fossil Fuel Water Boilers	Duty	Minimum Output Capacity	Maximum Output Capacity
	Gravity or forced convection terminals in the space, water coil in duct or air-handler.	1.00	1.40

Minimum and maximum capacity factors operate on the heating load produced by an accurate **Manual J** load calculation. Multiply a size factor by 100 to convert to a percentage. Refer to OEM guidance when a boiler is used for potable water heat, or snow melting.

Hot Water Coils	Duty	Minimum Factor	Maximum Factor	
			Two-position	Throttling
	Gravity or forced convection terminals in the space.	1.00	1.25	1.50
	Water coil in duct or air-handler.			

Minimum and maximum capacity factors operate on the heating load produced by an accurate **Manual J** load calculation. Multiply a size factor by 100 to convert to a percentage. Two-position = open-close valve; Throttling = Full modulating 2-way or 3-way valve.

Electric and Fossil Fuel Water Heaters	The space heating load is the **Manual J** load. The total load is the space heating load plus the potable water load. Refer to OEM guidance for selection and sizing guidance.
Dual Fuel Systems	Heat pump sizing rules apply, heating equipment sizing rules apply, see Section N2-11.
Ancillary Dehumidification	See Section N2-12. May allow +15,000 Btuh excess cooling capacity for cold winter climate.
Humidifiers (Section N2-13)	Minimum capacity ≥ humidification load, excess capacity dependent on smallest size available.
AHAM Cooling and Heat Pump Equipment	See Section N2-14 for sizing rules.
Direct Evaporative Cooling Equipment	See Section N2-15 for sizing rules.

Table extracted from ANSI/ACCA 3 Manual S – 2014, and section references are to that volume.

APPENDIX C | QUALITY ASSURED CONTRACTOR ELEMENTS

[This Appendix is not part of the Standard. It is merely informative and does not contain requirements necessary for conformance to the Standard. It has not been processed according to the ANSI requirements for a standard and may contain material that has not been subject to public review or a consensus process. Unresolved objectors on informative material are not offered the right to appeal at ACCA or ANSI.]

This Appendix highlights a subset of recommended business practices that support the company – and its employees – in consistently achieving the level of workmanship required by the QI Standard:

- ✓ Business Prerequisites
    - Licensing or Registration
    - Insurance
    - Code Requirements
    - Refrigerant Certifications, Training, and Equipment
    - Hazardous Materials Regulations
- ✓ Business Operations
    - Employment
    - Safety Programs
    - Fleet Management
    - Quality Installation
    - Quality Maintenance
    - Quality Restoration
    - Instrumentation/Measurement Tools
- ✓ Training & Certification
    - Continuing Education
    - Certification
- ✓ Customer Relations
    - Interactions with Building Owners and Homeowners
    - Warranties
    - Service Agreements

QA-1 BUSINESS PREREQUISITES

QA-1 focuses on the fundamental requirements for operating a legal contracting business.

QA-1.1 LICENSING OR REGISTRATION

The contractor shall possess all required statutory/regulatory licenses and other state or local registrations for the business as dictated by the requirements in each jurisdiction where the contractor does business. All such items are to be current.

QA-1.2 INSURANCE

The contractor shall carry at least the statutory levels of insurance and applicable bonds required by the appropriate jurisdictions where the company offers its services, as well as all applicable contractually required insurance. Such insurance coverage shall include, but is not limited to:

a) Liability,
b) Worker's compensation,
c) Company vehicles, and
d) Bonds.

QA-1.3 CODE REQUIREMENTS

All work performed by the contractor shall comply with all required state and local building codes, energy codes, and related regulations in each jurisdiction where the contractor does business, including, but not limited to:

a) HVAC equipment sizing,
b) HVAC selection,
c) HVAC installation,
d) HVAC servicing, and
e) HVAC maintenance.

QA-1.4 REFRIGERANT CERTIFICATIONS, TRAINING, AND EQUIPMENT

All technicians, or third-party subcontractors, who handle refrigerants are to recover/recycle refrigerants in compliance with EPA regulations (i.e., Section 608). The contractor is responsible for:

a) Use of operational Recover/Recycle equipment,
b) Use of operational evacuation equipment capable of maintaining a vacuum of at least 500 microns,
c) Ensuring company technicians who recover refrigerants, recycle refrigerants, or charge refrigerants to HVAC systems possess all required EPA refrigerant certifications (i.e., I, II, III or Universal),
d) Providing required recover/recycle equipment to company technicians who handle refrigerants,
e) Ensuring that pertinent technicians are trained in the correct use of recover/recycle equipment,
f) Ensuring that pertinent technicians are trained in the correct use of evacuation equipment,
g) Ensuring that company refrigerant records are kept in compliance with Section 608 EPA regulations.

QA-1.5 HAZARDOUS MATERIALS REGULATIONS

The contractor shall adhere to all applicable federal, state and local pollution codes and regulations related to handling hazardous materials, and will develop and comply with guidelines and policies for the safe and proper handling of hazardous materials and substances at the company workplace(s) and work sites, including:

a) Proper storage of hazardous materials and substances at the workplace,
b) Proper transportation of hazardous materials and substances to and from different sites,
c) Proper use of hazardous materials and substances by the company,
d) Proper disposal of hazardous materials and substances by the company,
e) Following proper procedures for treating and cleaning up discharges and accidental spills,
f) Ensuring material safety data sheets (MSDS) are used, and
g) Ensuring personnel use appropriate safety equipment.

QA-2   BUSINESS OPERATIONS

QA-2 focuses on business practices and procedures.

QA-2.1 EMPLOYMENT

The contractor shall perform reference and criminal background checks and ensure that all employees meet appropriate employment eligibility requirements.

QA-2.2 Safety Programs

The contractor shall ensure employees receive the appropriate type and level of safety training, including, but not limited to:

a) Fleet safety, and
b) Injury prevention.

QA-2.3 Fleet Management

The contractor shall ensure dedicated company vehicles meet federal, state and local laws and regulations and are properly maintained. Such compliance shall include, but not be limited to:

a) Ensuring that company vehicles are marked in accordance with legal requirements, and
b) Ensuring company vehicles are properly maintained in accordance with legal requirements.

QA-2.4 Quality Installation

The contractor shall ensure that HVAC equipment replacements and new equipment installations comply with ANSI/ACCA Standard 5 (*HVAC Quality Installation Specification*), and shall specifically develop and comply with policies which ensure that the contractor is following all Quality Installation ("QI") Specification requirements:

a) Ventilation requirements (per QI §3.1),
b) Heat-gain and heat-loss load calculations (per QI §3.2),
c) Properly-sized HVAC equipment (per QI §3.3),
d) Ground heat exchangers (per QI§3.4),
e) Properly matched systems (per QI §3.5),
f) Airflow through the indoor heat exchanger (per QI §4.1),
g) Waterflow through the indoor heat exchanger (per QI §4.2),
h) Refrigerant charge (per QI §4.3),
i) Electrical requirements (per QI §4.4),
j) Combustion equipment is "on-rate" (per QI §4.5),
k) Venting of combustion gases (per QI §4.6),
l) System operational and safety controls (per QI §4.7),
m) Air ducts are sealed (CFM) (per QI §5.1),
n) Room airflow (per QI §5.2),
o) Water flow (per QI §5.3),
p) Customer documentation (per QI §6.1), and
q) Owner and/or operator education (per QI §6.2).

QA-2.5 Quality Maintenance

The contractor shall develop and comply with policies and procedures ensuring that maintenance work performed is in accordance with ANSI/ACCA 4 QM Standard (*Maintenance of Residential HVAC Systems*) or ANSI/ASHRAE/ACCA/Standard 180 (*Standard Practices for Inspection and Maintenance of Commercial Building Systems*), and with OEM recommendations:

a) Inspections of the HVAC system,
b) Repairs and corrective actions, and
c) Inspection, repairs, cleanings, and other maintenance tasks.

QA-2.6 Quality Restoration

The contractor shall develop and comply with written policies for the relevant work undertaken regarding duct cleaning and other extraordinary system restoration work in accordance with ANSI/ACCA 6 QR Standard (*Restoring the Cleanliness of HVAC Systems*).

QA-2.7 Instrumentation/Measurement Tools

The contractor shall develop and comply with policies requiring that appropriate instrumentation/measurement tools are available for each service offered by the contractor. Further, the contractor shall maintain calibration and service records for instruments and test equipment that require calibration and maintenance.

QA-3 TRAINING & CERTIFICATION

QA-3 focuses on fundamental training and certification for HVAC contractors.

QA-3.1 Continuing Education

The contractor shall ensure that company personnel receive:

a) A minimum of 6 equivalent hours of application and technical training per year for each company salesperson/designer, and
b) A minimum of 12 equivalent hours of technical training per year; or technician maintains certification by an HVAC industry-recognized and accepted certification program (e.g., NATE).

QA-3.2 Certification

The contractor shall ensure employees maintain proper certification for relevant HVAC work undertaken, including, but not necessarily limited to:

a) All required federal, state and local certifications, and
b) Certification by NATE (or an accepted industry equivalent):
    a. For New construction: at least 25% of the company's start-up technicians.
    b. For Existing buildings: at least 25% of the company's technicians.

QA-4 CUSTOMER RELATIONS

QA-4 focuses on the manner in which a contractor addresses customer issues and concerns.

QA-4.1 Interactions with Building Owners and Homeowners

The contractor shall:

a) Identify potential defects or deficiencies in the HVAC system or the building,
b) Establish options to resolve any defects or deficiencies,
c) Confer with the building owner or builder over work to be performed, including equipment/material to be installed by the contractor,

d) Ensure that work performed materially meets the written contractual agreement between the customer and the company, and
e) Address customer complaints.

QA-4.2 WARRANTIES

Contractors offering warranties shall provide written documentation to the customer which includes, at a minimum, provisions addressing:

a) Scope of the warranty, including coverages and exclusions,
b) Whether the warranty is transferable,
c) The effective date of the warranty and any expiration dates, and
d) Contact information for resolution of warranty claims.

QA-4.3 SERVICE AGREEMENTS

Contractors offering service agreements shall provide customers written documentation which includes, at a minimum, provisions addressing:

a) Scope of the service agreement, including coverages and exclusions,
b) Whether the service agreement is transferable by either party,
c) The effective date and expiration date of the service agreement, and
d) Contractor contact information.

APPENDIX D | DEFINITIONS

[This Appendix is not part of the Standard. It is merely informative and does not contain requirements necessary for conformance to the Standard. It has not been processed according to the ANSI requirements for a standard and may contain material that has not been subject to public review or a consensus process. Unresolved objectors on informative material are not offered the right to appeal at ACCA or ANSI.]

AABC: Associated Air Balance Council.

ACCA: Air Conditioning Contractors of America.

Airflow:

Duct airflow balance: A condition that exists when the duct system has been properly designed and assembled (i.e., sizing, friction loss, balance dampers, etc.) to ensure that the correct volume of air (in CFMs) is delivered to each room or space. This term also is used to describe work associated with the measurement and adjusting of the airflow rates at various points in an air distribution system to provide correct airflow delivery to the rooms or spaces as prescribed during the design process.

Fan airflow: The total volume of air (in CFM) that exits the fan assembly or blower unit during operation at design conditions. [Fan airflow is a function of static pressure resistance presented by the duct system and any and all appliances and components connected within the subject duct system. A fan motor is designed to provide optimal airflow within a specified range of acceptable total static pressures. If a fan is installed in a duct system with appliances and components that exceed this total static pressure threshold, the fan cannot deliver proper airflow, and the system's capacity will be reduced. Variable-speed fans do not save energy when installed in duct systems that exceed total static pressure limits – they only provide more options for multi-stage equipment.]

Room airflow balance: A condition that exists when the airflow rate (CFM) entering a room or other enclosed space equals the airflow rate leaving the room, space or equipment.

AHRI: Air-Conditioning Heating, and Refrigeration Institute.

Amps (ampere; A): A unit of electric current.

ASHRAE: American Society of Heating, Refrigerating, and Air-Conditioning Engineers.

Blower: See fan.

Boiler: Vessel in which a liquid is heated with or without vaporization; boiling need not occur.

Bonding: (electrical ground) Connection to ground potential of a metal part on an appliance or component which may become energized by an electric fault, or develop a static charge.

Btu: British thermal unit, the amount of heat that must be added or removed to/from one pound of water to raise or lower its temperature one degree Fahrenheit.

Btuh or Btu/h: British thermal units added or removed per hour.

Built-up system: See system.

CEE: Consortium for Energy Efficiency.

CFM: Cubic feet per minute (ft^3).

Clearance*: Clearance for maintenance or repair: the distance between the item requiring maintenance and the closest interfering surface.

Combustion*: Chemical process of oxidation that occurs at a rate fast enough to produce heat and usually light either as a glow or flame.

Combustion analysis: Analysis of combustion as defined above.

Contractor*: The person or entity responsible for performing the work and identified as such in an owner-contractor agreement.

Control*: Device for regulation of a system or component in a normal and safe operation, manual or automatic; if automatic, the implication is that it is responsive to changes of pressure, temperature, or other variable whose magnitude is to be regulated.

Diffuser: An outlet designed to discharge air in a spreading pattern.

DOE: United States Department of Energy.

Duct modification: A change in the air distribution network that includes additions or deletions of duct runs or changes register/grille location(s). This does not include transitions at the air handler supply and return. Additionally, simple repairing or replacing damaged duct runs with like-size ducts are excluded from this definition.

EPA: United States Environmental Protection Agency.

ESP: External static pressure; external to the manufacturer's box.

Expansion coil: An evaporator (heat exchanger) constructed of bare or finned pipe or tubing in which direct expansion of liquid refrigerant occurs.

Fan*: Device for moving air by two or more blades or vanes attached to a rotating shaft.

> **Fan airflow:** See airflow.

Furnace*: 1. Part of a warm air heating system in which energy is converted to heat; **2.** Enclosed chamber or structure in which heat is produced, as by burning fuel, or by converting electrical energy.

Geothermal Heat Pump System: A geothermal heat pump system rejects heat to (in cooling mode) or extracts heat from (in heating mode) various ground resources, including the shallow surface of the Earth, ground water, surface water, etc. A geothermal heat pump system consists of the following three major components: a water source heat pump unit operable over an extended range of entering fluid temperatures, a ground heat exchanger, and a circulation system. Additionally, for ground water heat pump systems that do not use the direct expansion type of ground heat exchanger, a pump or pumps are usually needed to circulate the heat transfer medium (water or aqueous antifreeze solution) through the geothermal heat pump and the ground heat exchanger.

> **Geothermal Heat Pump**:** A geothermal heat pump uses the thermal energy of the ground or groundwater (or otherwise wasted resources) to provide residential or commercial space conditioning and/or domestic water heating. A geothermal heat pump normally consists of one or more factory-made assemblies that include indoor conditioning and/or domestic water heat exchanger(s), compressors, and a ground-side heat exchanger. A geothermal heat pump may provide space heating, space cooling, domestic water heating, or a combination of these functions and may also include the functions of liquid circulation, thermal storage, air circulation, air cleaning, dehumidifying or humidifying.

> **Ground Heat Exchanger:** The method by which heat is exchanged with the ground, groundwater, or surface water. Geothermal heat pumps may use any form of ground heat exchange, which includes horizontal, vertical, or submerged surface water closed loops; open loops using ground water, reclaimed water, or surface water; or direct refrigerant-to-ground or refrigerant-to-water heat exchange.

>> **Closed Loop:** A ground heat exchange method in which the heat transfer fluid is permanently contained in a closed piping system.

>> **Open Loop:** A ground heat exchange method in which the heat transfer fluid is part of a larger environment. The most common open loop systems use ground water, reclaimed water, or surface water as the heat transfer medium.

GPM: Gallons per minute.

Grille: A covering for an opening through which air passes.

Heat gain: The instantaneous flow (BTU/H) of sensible or latent heat entering the conditioned space or passing through a structural component. (A gain may or may not be equivalent to a space load, see Load Calculation).

Heat loss: The instantaneous flow (BTU/H) of sensible or latent heat leaving the conditioned space or passing through a structural component. (Losses are equivalent to space loads because thermal mass effects are ignored for winter heat loss calculations, see Load Calculation).

Heat pump*: Thermodynamic heating/refrigerating system to transfer heat in either direction. By receiving the flow of air or other fluid, a heat pump is used to cool or heat.

Cooling and heating heat pump*: System designed to utilize alternately or simultaneously the heat extracted at a low temperature and the heat rejected at a higher temperature for cooling and heating functions, respectively.

Heating heat pump*: Refrigerating system designed primarily to utilize the heat rejection from the system for a desired heating function.

HIA: Hydronics Industry Alliance.

HVAC: Heating, ventilating and air conditioning.

HVAC system*: A system that provides either collectively or individually the processes of comfort heating, ventilating, and/or air conditioning within, or associated with, a building.

HVACR: Heating, ventilating, air conditioning, and refrigeration.

IAQ: Indoor air quality.

IBR or I=B=R: AHRI training program for fossil fuel and hydronic appliances.

IFGC: International Fuel Gas Code.

IGSHPA: International Ground Source Heat Pump Association.

Installation file: The information left with or attached to the installed equipment. Owner's information.

Kilowatt-hour: Energy used in the marketing of electrical power. Units are Kilowatt (i.e., 1000 watts) per hour of usage.

Leakage:

Air leakage: The uncontrolled exchange of air between conditioned and unconditioned building spaces (or the interior and the outdoors) through unintended openings in the building envelope and/or unintended openings in duct runs through unconditioned spaces.

Distribution leakage: Leakage of the ambient air through the cracks and openings in supply and/or return ducts or the supply and/or return-side of HVAC equipment cabinetry.

Load calculation: A systematic method of evaluation that uses mathematical models (equations, databases, defaults and protocols) to estimate heat loss, sensible and latent heat gain, heating load, humidification load, sensible and latent cooling load, and related issues like infiltration, CFM minimum ventilation rate, month-hour temperature adjustments, building construction materials, building solar orientation, etc.

Block analysis: A load calculation approach where the total space heat loss/heat gain load imposed on equipment is determined on a space that may include more than one room or more than one zone.

Room-by-room analysis: A load calculation approach where the combined space heat loss/heat gain load imposed on equipment is determined on a room-by-room basis.

System load: Heat loss (sensible BTU/H) or heat gain (sensible and latent Btu/H) required for engineered ventilation, air or water distribution, relevant ancillary devices (e.g., blowers, motors, pumps), reheat and humidification.

Total load: Sensible and latent requirements in BTU/hr.

Magnehelic: A diaphragm-type pressure differential sensor with a direct reading gauge.

Manometer*: Instrument for measuring head or pressure; traditionally, a U-tube partially filled with a liquid, usually water, mercury, or manometer gage oil, so constructed that the difference in level of the liquid legs indicates the pressure exerted on the instrument.

Measurement*: 1. Act or result of determining the characteristics of some thing; **2.** Extent, capacity, or amount ascertained by measuring; **3.** System of measures.

Nameplate rating: Full-load continuous rating of a compressor, motor, or other equipment under specified conditions, as designated by the manufacturer, and usually indicated on an attached plate.

NATE: North American Technician Excellence.

NEBB: The National Environmental Balancing Bureau.

NEC: National Electrical Code.

NFGC: National Fuel Gas Code.

NGWA: National Ground Water Association.

OEM: Original equipment manufacturer.

On-rate (also known as fuel flow rate): Refers to the volume of fuel flowing into the combustion process at steady-state operation. Once the measured flow is corrected for temperature and altitude, the on-rate (for gas, rated in Btu/ft^3; for oil, rated in Btu/gal) can be established utilizing a fuel's heat content in Btu.

Piping*: 1. System of pipes for carrying fluids; **2.** Pipe or tube mains for interconnecting the various parts of a refrigerating system.

Pitot tube*: Small bore tube inserted perpendicular to a flowing stream with its orifice facing the stream to measure total pressure.

Refrigerant*: 1. In a refrigerating system, the medium of heat transfer which picks up heat by evaporating at a low temperature and pressure, and gives up heat on condensing at a higher temperature and pressure; **2.** (refrigerating fluid) Fluid used for heat transfer in a refrigerating system that absorbs heat at a low temperature and low pressure of the fluid and transfers heat at a higher temperature and a higher pressure of the fluid, usually involving changes of state of the fluid.

> **Charge: 1.** Actual amount of refrigerant in a closed system. **2.** Weight of refrigerant required for proper functioning of a closed system.
>
> **Reclaim:** (as in "reclaim refrigerant") To reprocess refrigerant to new conditions, by means which may include distillation; require chemical analysis of the contaminated refrigerant to determine that appropriate process specifications are met (This term usually implies the use of processes or procedures available only at a reprocessing or manufacturing facility).
>
> **Recover:** (as in "recover refrigerant") To remove refrigerant in any condition from a system and to store it in an external container without necessarily testing or processing it in any way.
>
> **Recycle:** (as in "recycle refrigerant") To clean refrigerant for reuse by oil separation and single or multiple passes through moisture absorption devices, such as filter driers with replaceable cores. This procedure is usually implemented at the field site or at a local service shop.

Safety/safeties: See control / safety control.

SHGC: Solar heat gain coefficient.

SMACNA: Sheet Metal and Air Conditioning Contractors National Association.

Steady-state: HVAC system operating in equilibrium (generally operating constantly for over 10 minutes) A system operating in a stable condition over time; where the change in one direction is balanced by change in another .

Subcooling: Removal of heat from a liquid when at a temperature lower than the saturation temperature corresponding to its pressure.

Superheat*: Extra heat in a vapor when at a temperature higher than the saturation temperature corresponding to its pressure.

System*: 1. Organized collection of parts united by regular interaction; **2.** A heating or refrigerating scheme or machine, usually confined to those parts in contact with a heating or refrigerating medium.

> **Control system:** See control.
>
> **Cooling system*:** Apparatus for lowering the temperature of a space or product to a specified temperature level.
>
> **Duct system:** A network of tubular or rectangular pipes and connectors (elbow, tees, branch fitting, and boot fitting) used to more air from one point to another.
>
> **Existing system:** One that has existed previously.
>
> **Geothermal heat pump system:** See geothermal heat pump.
>
> **Heating system*:** One in which heat is transferred from a source of energy through a distribution network to spaces to be heated.
>
> **Matched system:** The components of a split system are matched, rated, and have certified performance through the AHRI and/or CEE databases.

Multi-zone: HVAC system capable of handling variable loads from different sections of a building simultaneously or independently.

New system: One that has not previously been in existence.

Split system: (as in split system air conditioner) A two-component system with the condensing unit installed outside, remote from the evaporator section, which is installed in a conditioned space, and uses interconnecting refrigerant lines to connect the condensing unit to the evaporator.

Venting system: A venting system is designed in accordance with OEM and code requirements to direct flue or combustion gases from a fossil fuel burning appliance to the outside atmosphere.

TABB: Testing, Adjusting and Balancing Bureau.

Thermal envelope*: Elements of a structure that enclose conditioned spaces and control transmission of heat, air, and water vapor between the conditioned spaces and the exterior.

Unitary air conditioner*: One or more factory-made assemblies which normally may include an evaporator or cooling coil, a compressor and condenser combination, and may include a heating function. The equipment can be ducted or ductless; it can be a split-system or single package.

Voltage: Electric potential or potential difference expressed in volts.

Watts (W)*: A power term that reflects the work done or energy generated by one ampere induced by an emf of one volt ($P = EI = I^2R$).

Zoning*: 1. Division of a building or group of buildings into separately controlled spaces (zones), where different environmental conditions can be maintained simultaneously; **2.** Practice of dividing a building into smaller sections for control of heating and cooling (each section is selected so that one thermostat can be used to determine its requirements).

* Definition adapted from ASHRAE Terminology of Heating, Ventilation Air Conditioning & Refrigeration Second Edition 1991.

** Definition adapted from Energy Star Program Requirements for Geothermal Heat Pumps Partner Commitments Version 3 Definitions section.

APPENDIX E | PERTINENT HVAC BIBLIOGRAPHY & RESOURCES

[This Appendix is not part of the Standard. It is merely informative and does not contain requirements necessary for conformance to the Standard. It has not been processed according to the ANSI requirements for a standard and may contain material that has not been subject to public review or a consensus process. Unresolved objectors on informative material are not offered the right to appeal at ACCA or ANSI.]

AABC **Associated Air Balance Council (1518 K Street NW, Suite 503, Washington, DC, 20005; tel: 202/737-0202; www.aabc.com)**
- Commissioning Guideline, 2002
- Test and Balance Procedures, 2002

ACCA **Air Conditioning Contractors of America (2800 S. Shirlington Road, Suite 300, Arlington, VA, 22206; tel: 703/575-4477; www.acca.org)**

Manuals and Standards

Manual B®	Balancing and Testing of HVAC Systems, 2009
Manual CS®	Commercial Applications, Systems and Equipment, 1st ed., 1993
Manual D®	Residential Duct Systems, 2014
Manual J®	Residential Load Calculation, 8th ed., 2011
Manual N®	Commercial Load Calculation, 5th ed., 2008
Manual RS®	Comfort, Air Quality, and Efficiency by Design, 1997
Manual S®	Residential Equipment Selection, 2014
Manual SPS®	HVAC Design for Swimming Pools and Spas, 2010
Manual T®	Air Distribution Basics for Residential and Small Commercial Buildings, 1992
Manual Q®	Low Pressure, Low Velocity Duct System Design for Commercial Applications, 1990
Manual Zr®	Residential HVAC System Zoning, 2012
ACCA 4 QM - 2013	Maintenance of Residential HVAC Systems in One- and Two-Family Dwellings Less Than Three Stories, (pending ANSI review process), 2013
ACCA 6 QR-2015	Standard for Restoring the Cleanliness of HVAC Systems, 2015
ACCA 9 QIvp-2011	HVAC Quality Installation Verification Protocols, 2011
ACCA 12 QH-2014	Home Evaluation and Performance Improvement, 2014
ACCA 14 QMref-2015	Quality Maintenance of Commercial Refrigeration Systems, 2015

Other Documents
- Bob's House: Understanding the Residential HVAC Design Process, 2012
- HVAC Practices for Residential and Commercial Buildings: A Guide for Thermal, Moisture and Contaminant Control to Enhance System Performance and customer Satisfaction, 2003
- NIST Technical Note 1848: Sensitivity Analysis of Installation Faults on Heat Pump Performance, 2014
- Residential Duct Diagnostics and Repair, 2003
- Technical Bulletin: Ensuring ASHRAE 62.2-2013 Ventilation Compliance for Residential Structures, 2014
- Technician's Guide and Workbook for a Quality Installation, 2015
- Technician's Guide and Workbook for Home Evaluation and Performance Improvement, 2015

AHRI **Air Conditioning, Heating and Refrigeration Institute (4100 North Fairfax Drive, Suite 200, Arlington, VA, 22203; tel: 703/524-8800; www.ahrinet.org)**

Standards and Guidelines

Standard 210/240-2003	Unitary Air Conditioning and Air-Source Heat Pump Equipment, 2003
Standard 340/360-2004	Commercial and Industrial Unitary Air Conditioning and Heat Pump Equipment, 2004
Standard 700-2004	Specification for Fluorocarbon Refrigerants, 2004
Standard 740-98	Refrigerant Recovery/Recycling Equipment, 1998
Standard 880-98	Air Terminals, 1998
Guideline K-2005	Containers for Recovered Fluorocarbon Refrigerants, 2005
Guideline N-2002	Assignment of Refrigerant Color Containers, 2002
Guideline Q-2001	Content Recovery and Proper Recycling of Refrigerant Cylinders, 2001

Other Documents
- AHRI Product Certification directory/database: AHRI certification consists of manufacturers who voluntarily participate in independent testing to ensure that their product will perform according to published claims at specified controlled testing conditions. Go to http://www.ahridirectory.org/ahridirectory/pages/home.aspx for more information.
- Industry Recycling Guide (IRG-2), Handling and Reuse of Refrigerants in the US, 1994
- IBR (or I=B=R) Efficiency Rating Certified product directories provide free, downloadable lists of equipment and ratings tested under their various certification programs. See http://www.ahrinet.org/Content/GAMAIBRCertification_581.aspx.
- Residential Hydronic Heating Installation/Design (IBR Guide), 2009

ASHRAE — **American Society of Heating, Refrigerating and Air-Conditioning Engineers (1791 Tullie Circle, NE., Atlanta, GA; tel: 404/636-8400; www.ashrae.org)**

Standards and Guidelines

Standard 15-2013	Safety Standard for Refrigeration Systems, 2013
Standard 34-2009	Designation and Safety Classifications of Refrigerants, 2009
Standard 55-2013	Thermal Environmental Conditions for Human Occupancy, 2013
Standard 62.1-2013	Ventilation for Acceptable Indoor Air Quality, 2013
Standard 62.2-2013	Ventilation for Acceptable Indoor Air Quality in Low-Rise Residential Buildings, ANSI Approved, 2013
Standard 90.1-2013	Energy Standard for Buildings Except Low-Rise Residential Buildings, 2013
Standard 90.2-2007	Energy-Efficient Design of Low-Rise Residential Buildings, 2007
Standard 111-2008	Practices for Measurement, Testing, Adjusting, and Balancing of Building Heating, Ventilation, Air Conditioning and Refrigeration Systems, 2008
Standard 126-2008	Method of Testing HVAC Air Ducts, 2008
Standard 147-2013	Reducing the Release of Halogenated Refrigerants from Refrigerating and Air-Conditioning Equipment and Systems, 2013
Standard 152-2014	Method of Test for Determining the Design and Seasonal Efficiencies of Residential Thermal Distribution Systems, 2014
Standard 180-2012	Standard Practice for Inspection and Maintenance of Commercial HVAC Systems, 2012
Standard 183-2007	Peak Cooling and Heating Load Calculations in Buildings Except Low-Rise Residential Buildings, 2007 (RA 2011)
Guideline 0-2013	The Commissioning Process, 2013
Guideline 1.1-2007	The HVAC Commissioning Process, 2007
Guideline 4-2008	Preparation of Operating and Maintenance Documentation for Building Systems, 2008 (RA 2013)
Guideline 24-2008	Ventilation and Indoor Air Quality In Low-Rise Residential Buildings, 2008

Other Documents
- Handbook of Fundamentals, 2013
- Humidity Control; Harriman, Lew, Geoffrey W. Brundrett, and Reinhold Kittler
- Design Guide for Commercial and Institutional Buildings, 2001
- ASHRAE Terminology of Heating, Ventilation, Air Conditioning, & Refrigeration, 1991

BCA — **Building Commissioning Association (1400 SW 5th Avenue, Suite 700, Portland, OR 97201; tel: 877-666-2292; www.bcxa.org)**
- *The Building Commissioning Handbook*, 2nd Edition, John A. Heinz & Rick Casault

BPI — **Building Performance Institute (107 Hermes Road, Suite 110 Malta, NY 12020; 1-877-274-12741400; http://www.bpi.org/**
Various standards aimed at enhancing performance development of professional building performance analysis for: Air Conditioning and Heat Pumps, Building Envelope, Manufactured Housing, and Multifamily Buildings

APPENDIX E | PERTINENT HVAC BIBLIOGRAPHY & RESOURCES

CEE — **Consortium for Energy Efficiency (98 North Washington St., Suite 101, Boston, MA, 02114-1918; tel: 617-589-3949; www.cee1.org)**
The CEE/AHRI Verified Directory identifies a list of products (less than 65 Mbtuh) that the equipment manufacturers represent as meeting energy performance tiers established by the Consortium for Energy Efficiency (CEE) as part of the Residential Air Conditioner and Heat Pump Initiative and the High-Efficiency Commercial Air Conditioning Initiative. These initiatives make use of tiers to differentiate equipment on the basis of energy performance with a higher tier representing a higher level of claimed performance. Go to http://www.ceehvacdirectory.org/

IAPMO — **International Association of Plumbing and Mechanical Officials (5001 E. Philadelphia Street, Ontario, CA, 91761; tel: 909.472.4100; www.iapmo.org)**
— Uniform Mechanical Code, 2015
— Uniform Plumbing Code, 2015

ICC — **International Code Council (500 New Jersey Avenue, NW 6th Floor, Washington, DC 20001; tel: 888/422-7233; www.iccsafe.org)**
— International Building Code, 2015
— International Energy Conservation Code, 2015
— International Fire Code, 2015
— International Residential Code, 2015
— International Mechanical Code, 2015
— International Fuel Gas Code, 2015 (see Chapter 4, Tables 402.4(1) - 402.4 (33)

IGSHPA — **International Ground Source Heat Pump Association (374 Cordell South, Stillwater, OK 74078; tel: 405/774-5175; www.igshpa.okstate.edu)**
— Design and Installation Guide, 2009
— Residential and light Commercial Design and Installation Guide, 2003
— Closed-Loop Geothermal Systems, 2009
— Closed-Loop Geothermal Systems Slinky™ Guide, 2003
— Closed-Loop Geothermal Systems Soil and Rock Classification Field Manual, 2004
— Grouting for Vertical Geothermal Heat Pump Systems Engineering Design and Field Procedures Manual, 2000
— Closed-Loop Ground-Source Heat Pump Systems Installation Guide, 2007

NADCA — **National Air Duct Cleaning Association (1518 K Street, N.W., Suite 503, Washington, D.C., 20005; tel: 202/737-2926; www.nadca.com)**
— ACR Standard, 2013 Edition: Assessment, Cleaning & Restoration of HVAC Systems

NAIMA — **North American Insulation Manufacturers Association (44 Canal Center Plaza, Suite 310, Alexandria, VA 22314; tel 703/684-0084; www.naima.org)**
— Fibrous Glass Duct Construction Manual, 1st Edition, 1989.
— Fibrous Glass Duct Construction Standard, 2002
— Fibrous Glass Duct Liner Standard, 2002

NATE — **North American Technician Excellence (4100 North Fairfax Drive, Suite 210, Arlington, VA, 22203; tel: 703/276-7247; www.natex.org)**
NATE offers certifications tests for service and installation technicians to highlight relevant applied knowledge. Separate 'service' and 'installation' tests are given in the following specialty categories: air conditioning, distribution, air-to-air heat pump, gas heating (air), oil heating (air), hydronics gas, hydronics oil, light commercial refrigeration. Other credentials offered: ground source heat pumps, HVAC efficiency analyst

NEBB — **National Environmental Balancing Bureau (PO Box 2519, Liverpool, New York 13089; tel: 315-303-5559; www.nebb.org)**
— Procedural Standards for Testing, Adjusting, Balancing of Environmental Systems, 2005
— Procedural Standards for Building Systems Commissioning, 1999

NFPA	**National Fire Protection Association (Batterymarch Park, Quincy, MA, 02169, tel: 617/770-300; www.nfpa.org)**
	NFPA 54 — National Fuel Gas Code, 2015 (see Chapter 12, Tables 12.1 - 12.33)
	NFPA90a — Standard for the Installation of HVAC Systems 1999 Edition.
	NFPA 90b — Standard for the Installation of Warm Air Heating and Air-Conditioning Systems, 1999 Edition.
NGWA	**National Ground Water Association (601 Dempsey Road, Westerville, OH 43081; tel: 614/898-7791; www.ngwa.org)**
	– Guidelines for Construction of Loop Wells for Vertical Closed Loop Ground Source Heat Pump Systems, 3rd Edition, 2010
	– Development Methods for Water Wells, 1991
	– Ground Water Hydrology for Water Well Contractors, 1982
	– Guide for Using the Hydrogeologic Classification System for Logging Water Well Boreholes, 2006
	– Sealing Abandoned Wells, 1994
	– Basic Water Systems: A Pump and Hydraulic Training Manual, 2002
PECI	**Portland Energy Conservation Inc. (1400 SW 5th Ave, Suite 700, Portland, OR 97201; tel: 503/248-4636; www.peci.org)**
	– Model Commissioning Plan and Guide Specifications (v2.05); available for download
	– Operation and Maintenance Service Contracts: Guidelines for Obtaining Best-Practice Contracts for Commercial Buildings, available for download.
	– Practical Guide for Commissioning Existing Buildings, Tudi Hassl and Terry Sharp, 1999
PHCC	**Plumbing-Heating-Cooling Contractors-National Association (180 S. Washington Street, P.O. Box 6808, Falls Church, VA, 22046; tel: (703) 237-8100; www.phccweb.org)**
	– National Standard Plumbing Code, 2009
	– Variable Air Volume Systems, 1998
RESNET	**Residential Energy Services Network (P.O. Box 4561, Oceanside, CA 92052-4561; 1-800-836-7057; http://www.resnet.us/)**
	– Mortgage Industry National Home Energy rating Standard, 2009
	– RESNET National Standard for Home Energy Audits, 2005
	– ENERGY STAR Homes Building Option Package (BOP) Standard, 2000
	– RESNET Procedures for Certifying Residential Energy Efficiency Tax Credits, 2005
	– Rating and Home Energy Survey Ethics and Standards of Practice, 1996
	– RESNET Procedures for Verification of International Energy Conservation Code Performance Path Calculation Tools, 2004
	– RESNET Standards for Qualified Contractors and Builders, 2010
RPA	**Radiant Panel Association (Batterymarch Park, Quincy, MA, 02169, tel: 617/770-300; www.radiantpanelassociation.org)**
	– RPA Guidelines for the Design and installation of Radiant Heating and Snow Ice Melt Systems, 2010
	– Modern Hydronic Heating for Residential & light Commercial, 2003
RSES	**Refrigeration Service Engineers Society (1666 Rand Road, Des Plaines, IL, 60016-3552; tel: 847-297-6464; www.rses.org)**
	Various training manuals, self-study courses, classes and CDs to enhance the professional development of practitioners within the refrigeration sector.
SMACNA	**Sheet Metal and Air Conditioning Contractors' National Association (4201 Lafayette Center Drive, Chantilly, VA, 20151; tel: 703/803-2980; www.smacna.org)**
	– Building Systems Analysis & Retrofit Manual, 1995
	– Fibrous Glass Duct Construction Standards, 2003
	– Fire, Smoke and Radiation Damper Installation Guide for HVAC Systems, 2002
	– HVAC Air Duct Leakage Test Manual, 1985
	– HVAC Duct Systems Inspection Guide, 2000
	– HVAC Duct Construction Standards, Metal and Flexible, 2005
	– HVAC Systems Commissioning Manual. 1994, 1st ed.

APPENDIX E | PERTINENT HVAC BIBLIOGRAPHY & RESOURCES

- HVAC Systems – Duct Design, 1990
- HVAC Systems Testing, Adjusting & Balancing. 2002, 3rd Edition
- IAQ Guidelines for Occupied Buildings Under Construction. 1995, 1st Edition
- Rectangular Industrial Duct Construction Standards, 2004
- Round Industrial Duct Construction Standards, 1999

TABB **Testing, Adjusting and Balancing Bureau (8403 Arlington Blvd, Suite 100, Fairfax, VA, 22031; tel: 703/299-5646; www.tabbcertified.org)**
- Commissioning Guideline, 2002
- Test and Balance Procedures, 2002

UL **Underwriters Laboratories Inc. (333 Pfingsten Road, Northbrook, IL, 60062; tel: 847-272-8800; www.ul.com)**

Standard UL-181	Standard for Safety Factory-Made Air Ducts and Air Connectors, 2013
Standard UL-181A	Standard for Safety Closure Systems for Use with Rigid Air Ducts and Air Connectors, 2013
Standard UL-181B	Standard for Safety Closure Systems for Use with Flexible Air Ducts and Air Connectors, 2013